# MindRight: Navigate the Noise

## ALSO BY KEVIN STACEY

### TimeRight:

Take Control of your 1440 minutes for Maximum Effectiveness and Sanity

### MessageRight:

Take Control of your Email, Texts, and IMs for Maximum Efficiency and Sanity

# MindRight:
## Navigate the Noise

How to Deal with Your Internal Fake News
for Success, Resiliency, Mental Toughness,
and Peace of Mind

**Kevin Stacey, MBA**
TrainRight Media

*For Olivia, Zachary and Colin,*
*with special thanks to Brian*

Ordering Information/Quantity sales:
Special discounts are available on quantity purchases by
corporations, associations, and others. For details,
contact the publisher at the address below.

First Edition (v.1.2)
Published by TrainRight Media

ISBN-13: 978-0-578-48600-0
ISBN-10: 0-578-48600-8


TrainRight Media
Division of TrainRight, Inc.
207 Fruit St
Hopkinton, MA 01758 USA
1-800-603-7168
www.TrainRightInc.com
info@trainrightinc.com

# Table of Contents

# 1. Introduction

Welcome to MindRight: Navigate the Noise. I'm so glad you're investing the time to read it. Getting your mind right and navigating its noise is crucial for your life's success, enjoyment, and peace of mind. I hope it's not breaking news to you that there's extensive noise going on in your mind. It's part of being human. In fact, most researchers agree that we think, on average, over 50,000 thoughts a day. That's a lot of noise. Realistically, the noise is never going to stop. Unfortunately, much of what we think about is negative, counter-productive, or not based on reality. However, every thought we entertain creates a physical reaction, affects our outputs and performance, and if it's emotionally charged enough, creates our future.

Not skillfully navigating the noise and letting it stay there unrecognized, unchallenged, and unabated in its needling of us is dangerous and devastating at many levels. Simply put, being in your head too much and overthinking prevents you from fully living.

Now more than ever, people long for solutions and seek more satisfaction, peace of mind and success. Even a 10% increase in any of these areas would be a great relief. Although many of us in this country seem to view ourselves as the most advanced in the world, we're certainly not the healthiest or happiest.

In this country we declared the pursuit of happiness as a fundamental right, but lately that pursuit has proven elusive. According to the World Health Organization, the US is one of the least happy, and by far the most anxious, of all developed countries. Our life expectancy is ranked one of the lowest of high-income countries.[1] Suicide rates are at a 30-year high. This is despite the fact that we have only 5% of the world's population but we consume almost half of the world's prescription drugs.[2] Deaths of despair, including early deaths from substance dependency and chronic liver disease, have risen at alarming rates and are becoming a national crisis.

I was introduced to the brain, neuroscience and psychology while working in clinical healthcare as a magnetic resonance imaging technologist (MRI) in the mid-1990s. I performed anatomical brain scans and grew fascinated by the anatomy and function. For the rest of the body, it was easy to figure out how most of it worked. But the brain, that's where the mystery is. I studied the various images I took, trying to figure out how it all worked, and how thoughts were created. Once I discovered that there is electrical activity going on, I was hooked. This drove me to start researching the brain in both formal and informal settings.

The brain is an astonishingly complex organ and our scientific understanding of it is constantly evolving. There are billions of neurons that receive, process, and transmit information through electrical and chemical signals. There are numerous types of these chemicals, called neurotransmitters, all with distinct functions. There is a lot going on, and a lot that can go wrong, in our not-so-simple brains.

In our complex world, we need to make things simpler. There is a deluge of information available to us, and there is enough over-analyzing, overthinking, over explaining, and analysis paralysis going on. Therefore, I will keep the language and concepts in this book straightforward, easy to grasp, and easy to apply. As John Stout says, "Simplicity is the first cousin of contentment."

This book is not intended to address major, severe, or clinical mental health illnesses or trauma. These are serious, scary, and incapacitating health conditions that are sometimes accompanied by a chemical imbalance or other structural changes in the brain. You can't think or navigate your way out of mental illness; there's no shame in it, no reason to look for blame, and it's necessary to get proper evaluation and treatment. However, there is quite a range of severity with these conditions, and the mental noise and mental processes are where it begins and has quite an impact on them. More on that in the next chapter.

Rather than debilitating circumstances, I'm addressing the self-created and self-inflicted pain from our mental noise that can easily become a constant undercut of anxiety and stress that depletes your peace of mind. It's like a thousand paper cuts. It can drive you to drink or otherwise self-medicate. It prevents you from performing at your best, reaching your full potential, undermines your self-confidence, and can cause you to second guess, question and doubt yourself. It and can cause you to take yourself too seriously and become overly self-absorbed. It can increase insecurity and cause you to be too invested in seeking the approval of others. Approval addiction is more prevalent than people realize, and most aren't even aware that they're immersed in it. The noise can also hold you back from taking risks, enjoying the success you deserve, and cause you to have a distorted view of yourself wherein you don't see the strengths that the people around you see in you. It doesn't matter what the facts and circumstances are in our life, or if everyone arounds us thinks it's crazy, or if there is no logical reason for the way we think or have the anxiety we have. Our thoughts, or self-talk, create our feelings and moods. What we feel is what's true for us. As Henry David Thoreau told us, "Most men lead lives of quiet desperation." Not outwardly desperate, not unable to function, just not functioning at your best or being the best version of yourself.

I know that the noise our brains create is seductive and wants your attention; it wants to draw you into it. I know how exhausting it is when you engage with it too much. It wasn't until I was in my mid 30's that I really started to recognize my noise for what it is and began to learn how to navigate it. My normal for a long time was being needled by it and letting it cause me angst. I was allowing myself to be a victim of my own thoughts. A propensity to overanalyze and think too much left me to feel withdrawn, stressed, or anxious.

Looking back, I could have lived with a lot more joy and fun, and less torment. I probably had a low to mid-level of anxiety throughout most of my life. I refuse to feel bad about it because that was my path. None of them were mistakes; these were the lessons I needed to learn, and without them, I wouldn't be where or who I am today. I can't turn back the clock and neither can you. The lessons we learn from the past are more valuable than gold.

Nowadays, having my family and three kids who are in, or rapidly approaching, middle school helps with the resolve to think differently. Seeing their rapid evolution just reinforces how precious the time you have is and how quickly it goes by. You can't get it back and you don't get a second chance. I absolutely don't want to have the regret of not being fully there and present with them, of being preoccupied with the garbage that my brain can present to me and overthinking things. I also believe that how satisfied the parents are with their lives is one of the top indicators on how healthy children will ultimately turn out.

It's unfortunate that it's so self-inflicted. This is more than baggage and more like a ball and chain. The phrases 'brain bullies', or 'brain demons', are very accurate descriptions. It's that deceiving inner critic that does a lot of damage, frequently in a stealth fashion.

Unfortunately, what it takes for many people to become aware of this and resolve to stop it is a 'sudden wake-up call'. This is an event that gives you an epiphany of perspective, usually a major health crisis, a significant loss, or close call of losing something irreplaceable. Once you get the perspective of a real crisis, it's easier to see the self-created ones for what they are, and to be able to say, "I can't believe I wasted so much energy for so long fretting over that, because now I can see in the grand scheme of things how unimportant and ridiculous it is."

Teddy Roosevelt said it the best when he told us, "If you could kick the person in the pants responsible for most of your trouble, you wouldn't sit for a month." But what part of you would it be, that would be most responsible for your trouble? It wouldn't be in your pants. It wouldn't be physical— it would be mental, in your mind. Our private internal dramas, dialogues, and mental noise can do enough damage, so instead of blaming ourselves, most of us need to be kinder to ourselves and redirect our wrath and fury towards this noise. It's easier when we separate it from ourselves and see the noise for what it is.

"Two Wolves" is an old Cherokee parable. A Cherokee elder is teaching his grandson about life. "A fight is going on inside me," he said to the boy. "It's a terrible fight and it is between two wolves. One is evil— he is anger, envy, sorrow, regret, greed, arrogance, self-pity, guilt, resentment, inferiority, lies, false pride, superiority and ego." He continued, "The other is good— he is joy, peace, love, hope, serenity, humility, kindness, benevolence, empathy, generosity, truth, compassion, and faith. The same fight is going on inside you— and inside every other person, too." The grandson thought about it for a minute and then asked his grandfather, "Which wolf will win?" The old Cherokee smiled and quietly replied, "The one you feed." Such a powerful example that reminds us we can't feed the negative noise with our attention.

It also helps to know that everyone must deal with this since it's part of the human condition. It doesn't mean that we're deficient in any way. It helps when celebrities open up about their challenges as it breaks down the stigma and increases awareness.

Reese Witherspoon, who announced that she was sexually assaulted by a director at the age of 16, revealed in People Magazine that she feels fear in her life "all the time", but the actress says she's come up with a way to combat those bad feelings when they occur. "I see fear (the noise) as this little creature that lives in my life all the time, and I can either pay it attention and not get anything done or I can march ahead and ignore it. Sometimes I just have to jump two feet into a cold pool and go, 'OK, I believe in myself enough, I know I work hard. I know I can always bet on myself.' " 3

Theo Epstein, the baseball executive who led both the Chicago Cubs to end their 108-year championship drought, and Boston Red Sox to break their 86-year championship drought, is someone whose success I've admired. I was fascinated to read an in-depth featured story on him in ESPN (the magazine). In it, he revealed his struggles with stress, and shared how, at one point, it was turning into physical symptoms, as his neck hurt so bad he couldn't turn his head more than a few degrees.

What really got my attention was when Epstein said that the main battle he fights is against himself— and the things inside his own head. "If I let my brain follow its path unfettered, it would be kinda ugly," he says. "I learned simple mental health things: self-talk, breathing."4 This is a powerful and insightful statement, and a great example of what I'm getting at in this book. Most people would point to external circumstances as the source of stress, but he understands that stress is created in the brain. That is more than half the battle—to just grasp that. Most of us simply rotate from one crisis to the next. When one gets solved another one arises. All the while we feel anxious about things. But we never once consider that it's not the various situations that cause the anxiety, it's how we think. It at least must be in the equation. Any success we achieve is despite our mental noise, not because of it.

In professional sports, it's easy to see the connection between successfully navigating your mental noise and confidence and performance. In fact, most professional teams now employ mental skills coaches. The New England Patriots have a sign in their facility to remind personnel to "ignore the noise". Over the years that's become one of their iconic trademarks, and some would argue a contributor to their success. The emphasis they place on this just reinforces how crucial it is to successfully navigate your noise and how harmful it can be if you don't. Imagine the distractions that a professional team would be challenged by. For the sports media that covers the team, they need good ratings to be successful; to get good ratings they need to be provocative and stir up controversy and speculation about the team. It could be criticism for mediocre performance, speculation about trades or being replaced by younger draft picks, rumors of conflicts, or other negative topics. Yes, learning to ignore external noise is crucial. But what about the internal noise? That's even more challenging to navigate and can cause enough angst.

Nowadays, as a corporate consultant looking at ways to help others reach their full potential and meet their goals, I use this knowledge to help others be more successful, and I'm convinced that this is where the room for improvement is located. Regardless of your industry— sports, sales, management, etc., a lot of forward-thinking companies I work with are turning to different forms of mindset training to improve their bottom line. Fortune 500 companies are most definitely using the lessons gleaned from neural and behavioral sciences to help improve the way individuals think and therefore act. Most of us aren't judged at work by how much weight you can lift, but rather how much information we can process and quality decisions we can make. It's not just about business acumen, it's about managing our biology. Since we're using our brain, and we really are corporate athletes, we must ask ourselves: What we are doing to train our brains?

Most employers grasp that they're probably not getting the full mental capacity or focus of their staff. That's understandable on many levels since we're human, complicated, and the different aspects of our life spill over and affect the others, but it also can be addressed and improved upon.

An organization thrives or fails based on thousands of moment- to-moment actions, reactions and decisions. And it really comes down to the way individuals think about themselves and their jobs. A peak performance mindset is one in which your mind is functioning at its highest level, so you can perform at your highest level.

Thus, as we begin this book, here are some baseline self-awareness questions to ask yourself:

How often do you think about *what* you think about? How loud is your noise? How incessant is it? How much credence do you give it, or do you have a healthy skepticism with it? To what extent do you control it, or does it control you? Do you have an appreciation of the overwhelming, all-encompassing impact it has on your life? Do you feel as though you think too much? Just because you think something, must you dwell on it? How much does it rile you up? What is your relationship with your noise? Is it front page news? Is it even worthy of pondering?

Regardless of your circumstances, getting your mind right and navigating your noise is one of the best things you can do. We can't change a lot of circumstances that life throws at us. But working on ourselves, how we respond, and navigating our internal dialogue is a brilliant investment of effort.

To end this introduction, here are some of my favorite quotes on thinking and the noise. Mark which ones resonate with you:

"I think and think and think, I've thought myself out of happiness one million times, but never once into it." — Jonathan Safran Foer

"We are addicted to our thoughts. We cannot change anything if we cannot change our thinking." — Santosh Kalwar

"Stop thinking and end your problems." — Lao Tzu

"Whether you think you can, or you think you can't— you're right."
— Henry Ford

"The greatest weapon against stress is our ability to choose one thought over another" — William James

"Today I escaped anxiety. Or no, I discarded it, because it was within me, in my own perceptions— not outside." — Marcus Aurelius

"We become what we think about." — Earl Nightingale

"Choose not to be harmed and you won't feel harmed. Don't feel harmed and you haven't been." — Marcus Aurelius

"Change your thoughts and you change your world."
— Norman Vincent Peale

"What you think, you become. What you feel, you attract. What you imagine, you create." — Gautama Buddha

"Rule your mind or it will rule you." — Horace

"There is nothing either good or bad, but thinking makes it so."
— William Shakespeare, Hamlet

"We cannot solve our problems with the same level of thinking that created them." — Albert Einstein

"I've had a lot of worries in my life, most of which never happened."

— Mark Twain

"Very little is needed to make a happy life; it is all within yourself, in your way of thinking." — Marcus Aurelius

"It is hard to fight an enemy who has outposts in your head."
— Sally Kempton

"If you realize that you have enough, you are truly rich." — Lao Tzu

"Simple can be harder than complex: You have to work hard to get your thinking clean to make it simple. But it's worth it in the end because once you get there, you can move mountains." — Steve Jobs

"The problem isn't that Johnny can't read. The problem isn't even that Johnny can't think. The problem is that Johnny doesn't know what thinking is; he confuses it with feeling." — Thomas Sowell

"Five percent of the people think; ten percent of the people think they think; and the other eighty-five percent would rather die than think."
— Thomas A. Edison

"Always aim at complete harmony of thought and word and deed. Always aim at purifying your thoughts and everything will be well."
— Mahatma Gandhi

"If you are distressed by anything external, the pain is not due to the thing itself, but to your estimate of it; and this you have the power to revoke at any moment." — Marcus Aurelius

"A thought is harmless unless we believe it. It's not our thoughts, but our attachment to our thoughts, that causes suffering." — Byron Katie

"Whatever we expect with confidence becomes our own self-fulfilling prophecy." — Brian Tracy

"Have you envisioned wild success lately?" — David Allen

"Whatever we plant in our subconscious mind and nourish with repetition and emotion will one day become a reality." — Earl Nightingale

"If you believe that feeling bad or worrying long enough will change a past or future event, then you are residing on another planet with a different reality system." — William James

"Whenever two people meet, there are really six people present. There is each man as he sees himself, each man as the other person sees him, and each man as he really is." — William James

"Judge a man by his questions rather than by his answers." — Voltaire

"Folks are usually about as happy as they make up their minds to be." — Abraham Lincoln

"Never underestimate your power to change yourself; never overestimate your power to change others." — Wayne Dyer

"Find the good. It's all around you. Find it, showcase it and you'll start believing it." — Jesse Owens.

"Learn how to be happy with what you have while you pursue all that you want." — Jim Rohn

"Consult not you fears but your hopes and dreams. Think not about your frustrations, but about your unfilled potential. Concern yourself not with what you tried and failed in, but with what is still possible for you to do." — Pope John XXIII

# 2. The Noise and Mental Health

Mental health challenges are more common and a growing issue in our society. Statistics on prevalence are always changing, but one from the National Institute for Mental Health has it that approximately 1 in 5 adults in the US experiences a form of mental illness in a given year. I've seen others that have it as substance use disorders and mental illness combined affect 1 out of every 3 adults in this country. This is despite the huge increase of people taking prescription antidepressants. In the early 1980's only 1 in 50 Americans were taking them, now it's 1 in 9.[5] The opioid crisis seems to have opened some minds and moved things to the forefront of the national conversation. Globally, depression is increasing worldwide and is now the leading cause of global mental and physical disability.

Our younger population has been especially affected. Record numbers of college students are seeking treatment for depression and anxiety, and schools can't keep up. A class on happiness, called Psychology and the Good Life, was recently named the most popular class in the over 300-year history of Yale University. According to a recent American College Health Association's survey, 61% of college students said they had felt overwhelming anxiety within the last 12 months and 39% saying they felt so depressed that it was difficult for them to function.[6] Another study surveyed 67,000 college students and found that 20 percent of all students surveyed thought about suicide, and 9 percent had attempted it.[7] Suicide is currently the 2nd-leading cause of death among US teenagers. It seemed in the 1960's young people were taking drugs to zone out and relax, but nowadays they're taking performance-enhancing drugs such as Adderall to address self-imposed pressure to compete, improve and be perfect. The millennial generation is now largely known as the burnout generation.

There are so many officially recognized disorders that it's easier to think of them in three main groupings: internalizing (most commonly, depression and anxiety); externalizing (addiction, or anti-social behavior problems); and psychosis (with its characteristic symptoms often bracketed under the label of schizophrenia).

I've had to deal with it myself as bi-polar disorder runs in my family, and I've had to take three of my family members to emergency mental health to attempt to get them stabilized. A few times they accepted the help and agreed to be admitted, and a few times they demanded to be released. The facility had to let them go since they couldn't prove the patients were a danger to themselves or others. That's the threshold needed to hold them without consent. It's a frustrating situation. You want to help the people you care about but can't force them to do what's necessary to take care of themselves.

Mental health issues are immensely frustrating for numerous reasons. First of all, some people don't accept it and can be very dismissive and non-empathic to the plight of folks struggling with them. They can make statements similar to, "Just get over it… get with the program… just smile more… or even, just decide to be happy." It's not a visible illness or injury; it can be harder for some people to accept that it is in fact a real health challenge. Major depression is debilitating. Thankfully, I've never been afflicted by it, but from what I've been told it is frightening. My best friend from high school has been struggling with it on and off for a few years. He tells me it feels like your body is full of concrete, making it nearly impossible to find the strength to get out of bed. He's been unable to work for an extended period of time, and he's told me he'd prefer to have cancer or another illness that people could empathize with. He avoids running into coworkers while out shopping or in public. He suspects some think there's nothing wrong with him and he's just trying to milk the system.

Overall, it does appear that the stigma of mental health issues is abating. The more that people talk about it, the more it helps. The most decorated Olympian of all time, Michael Phelps, recently shared his struggles with depression and that he contemplated suicide after his second drunk-driving arrest in 2014. He hopes his partnership with Talkspace, which helps connect those in need with therapists through a computer, tablet or smartphone, will help those who are reluctant to seek out help, or would avoid in-person help, or may not have the financial means.

He is now dedicating a large portion of his time to promoting mental health awareness and said, "The biggest thing is always communicating. That's just something that's so powerful. It's getting it out so it's not sitting inside of you. Because if it sits inside of you it just eats at you. For me, I carried a lot of stuff along for 20-plus years, and I wish I didn't. Never isolate, never shut down," he said. "Always open up, just ask questions, and talk. Always remember that it's okay to not be okay." [8]

This is helpful, and things may be moving in the right direction, but that doesn't change the fact some people need to be educated, suspend their skepticism, and open their minds. An effective support system is essential for people struggling with these challenges. They shouldn't have to spend their energy trying to get the people who should be supporting them the most, to become educated and understanding.

Another frustration is it's often difficult to find the correct diagnosis and effective treatment plan. That can take years. With most radiology I performed, the result was instantaneous. The brain is very different. That's why a manual is needed (the DSM) for mental health professionals to use as a guide. For anxiety disorders alone, there are currently 11 different ones listed in the DSM and they are being diagnosed in rising numbers. Anxiety and stress can also present themselves as ADHD symptoms. The diagnostic criteria are complex and just not as straightforward as many other health issues.

It can take weeks or months to get an appointment with a mental health provider. In some parts of the country it's easier to buy a gun than to get mental health care. Insurance complications, reimbursement issues and paperwork hurt access. Some of the best providers don't even want to deal with insurance anymore and will only accept direct out-of-pocket payments from patients. Often, prescribers only offer very brief appointment windows, and they are not the same person who will also offer counseling.

Treatments can be frustrating. Everyone's brain chemistry is different and responds differently. For depression alone, there are currently 17 different medications available. It's not uncommon for there to be some trial and error and for patients to need to do their own research. It may take several prescribers to find one who will work with you and try different medication combinations to find what works best. You don't even know if it's having any effect for a few weeks since most psychotropic medications take that amount of time before they begin to work. In addition, some estimates have it that at least twenty percent of people with depression don't respond to any antidepressant medications.

The exciting news is genetic testing is now available to rule out which medications will be ineffective or have side effects, known as pharmacogenomics. How we respond to a medication depends on our genes, and an analysis of our DNA gives information that saves so much time and heartache. It's more common in cancer treatment and just now becoming more widespread for psychoactive drugs. One version of the test is called GeneSight. It's a simple, 10-second cotton-swab from the inside of your cheek to get a saliva sample. You get a report listing all the known medications for depression, anxiety, and ADHD, etc. divided into three categories: which ones you'll respond fully to and get the full effect from; which medications you'll only partially respond to; and which ones you'll have no response to and will likely get side effects from. It can also be determined if a person has a version of the MTHFR gene mutation, which puts you at a higher risk for several mental health challenges.

There have been some new treatments introduced. Recently approved by the FDA, ECT— or Electroconvulsive therapy, formerly called shock therapy— uses an electric current to attempt to treat some serious disorders.

Transcranial Magnetic Stimulation (TMS) has magnetic pulses that pass through the skull and causes small electrical currents that stimulate nerve cells in a targeted brain region. A powerful magnet placed on the head, where motion is controlled, can even result in a patient's arm to suddenly and involuntarily lash out.

Cranial Electrotherapy Stimulation (CES) delivers a mild electrical current through wearing ear clips for 20-60 minutes a day while doing normal activities to attempt to treat anxiety, insomnia, and depression without prescription drugs.

A new type of drug that appears to be on the horizon to treat depression, anxiety, PTSD, and other mood disorders along with nerve pain is ketamine. It's been used as a powerful anesthetic since the 1960s, and illegally as the club drug Special K. It's given at much lower doses to patients who have tried two or more medications without success. Initial results are compelling, showing the drug works quickly on people who haven't gotten better with other treatments and makes dramatic improvements in mood. The FDA has granted two ketamine-based drugs breakthrough therapy status and fast-tracked them to market. One of these is given by infusion. The other, Spravato, is a nasal spray administered by an approved health care provider in a doctor's office or medical clinic. Unlike traditional antidepressants, which work by shifting the balance of brain chemicals like serotonin and dopamine, ketamine is thought to change the way neurons communicate with each other. This drug is part of an emerging competitive theory about psychiatric disease— that it's less about chemical imbalance and more about structural changes in the brain or genetic make-up, mostly related to chronic stress overexciting and damaging neurons. Traumatic brain injury is also a factor. Ketamine's key effect is to block glutamate receptors, which are the brain's "go" signal. This in turn reduces calcium flow into neurons, reducing the risk of the neurons shrinking or self-destructing.

There is also evidence and ongoing studies that ketamine might work to prevent mental health issues, as a kind of vaccine. The first evidence came from the battlefield, as US soldiers injured in Iraq were treated with various anesthetics, including ketamine. Of 25,000 service members wounded in Iraq between 2002 and 2005, soldiers treated with ketamine got PTSD about half as often— even though they had more severe burns requiring more surgeries and longer hospital stays.[9]

"Ketamine is potentially the most exciting development in my lifetime for the treatment of mood disorders, but there is still a way to go before this is ready for prime time," says Gerard Sanacora, MD, PhD, director of the Depression Research Program at Yale University. Doctors don't know much about the long-term effects of ketamine because it hasn't been studied over long periods of time. Larger studies need to be done on ketamine, but these can cost millions of dollars. Because ketamine is a generic drug, pharmaceutical companies can't patent it and earn their money back.

Zulresso, a form of brexanolone, is the first drug approved by the FDA to specially treat postpartum depression. This debilitating condition is not talked about enough. It's the most common complication of pregnancy, affecting as many as one in seven women during or after pregnancy. Brexanolone is a synthetic form of allopregnanolone, a hormone produced by progesterone in the brain that may help ease depression and anxiety by dampening neural activity. The drug works very quickly, providing immediate relief, lasting a month, within 48 hours— a significant improvement over currently available antidepressants. To date, it's only available as an extremely expensive infusion delivered over 60 hours, requiring a stay in a medical center. A similar pill version, which would be easier for patients and less expensive, is currently in clinical trials.

A new twist on the common treatment of exposure therapy uses virtual reality to take it a step further by allowing patients to interact with realistic situations to reduce their anxiety. One program, developed for college students by Headset Health in partnership with the Columbia University Clinic for Anxiety and Related Disorders, allows to students to slip on a virtual reality headset and come face-to-face with a variety of anxiety-inducing simulations— from a professor unwilling to budge on a deadline, to an inconsiderate roommate who has littered his dorm room with food and piles of dirty clothes. There seems to be a lot of potential to use this type of technology for a variety of applications in the future.

Neurofeedback also uses technology in the form of real-time scans to attempt to teach patients to change how they think. Patients go into a functional magnetic resonance imaging scanner and are told to conjure memories or look at pictures while their brains are scanned. The activity of certain brain regions is analyzed, and patients see visual representations of their brain activity almost in real time—often presented in the form of a colored bar or thermometer. Based on what their brains are doing, they are told to enhance or suppress that activity by focusing on different memories or pictures to change how they're feeling. The goal is to train their brain like they would train their muscles when they want to be fit. It's currently expensive but its use may become more widespread as costs decrease.

Eye Movement Desensitization and Reprocessing (EMDR), is another newer, nontraditional form of treatment that I've had good success with. More on this in chapter 12.

Some other treatments that are helpful include counseling, or talk therapy, psychotherapy, cognitive behavioral therapy, mindfulness-based approaches to include meditation, exercise, and bibliotherapy using books like this one to provide guidance. There are many different tools that can address and lessen the severity of these challenges. As long as the conditions are not "full blown", severe, or clinical. New advancements should hopefully continue to evolve and improve as technology advances.

Sadly, some people don't seek help. According to the Anxiety and Depression Association of America, only about one-third of the estimated 44 million Americans suffering from anxiety disorders receive treatment.

A certain amount of worry is normal. When it turns into a permanent cloud that you can't seem to shake, is persistent and excessive, treatment is warranted. There shouldn't be any shame or hesitation asking for help and seeking treatment.

Alcoholism, which is more prevalent in men, begins for many as a self-medicating coping mechanism to deal with anxiety, panic and depression. This is likely because it is viewed as less socially acceptable for men to express these emotions and they avoid seeking help. Some cultures (one I've been told of repeatedly is Latin cultures) don't do well in acknowledging mental health challenges, seeking help and supporting those afflicted.

It is important to recognize that there is a range of severity and symptoms of mental health challenges. We can all, at times, experience various symptoms of various disorders, so severity and frequency are paramount.

How you navigate your noise has an enormous effect, especially with internalizing issues such as anxiety and depression. It's easy to think of anxiety as an active arousal. However, depression is also a state of high arousal, characterized by loud mental noise that stirs you up, prevents you from getting restorative sleep, which then leads to more nervous exhaustion. The apathy and exhaustion seen in people struggling with depression is a consequence of too much arousal, and the way the body and mind respond to this noise.

Depression and anxiety can best be understood as two sides of a single coin. "Everyone who's depressed is also anxious, but not everyone who's anxious is depressed," says Barlow.[10] Depression is so devastating because of the accompanying feelings of sadness, worthlessness, excessive guilt, tiredness, irritability, difficulty sleeping, and loss of interest in once-pleasurable activities.

We need to be reminded that the way we think and respond to situations creates the emotions we feel. It's also important to grasp that the emotional states we're in affect the chemicals which are released in our brains. Not only do our thoughts and emotions affect chemical composition and stress hormones like cortisol, but the chemical composition affects thoughts and emotions. You could argue what comes first— chemical imbalances, genetic makeup or structural changes that contribute to negative thinking, or negative thoughts which direct the chemicals to the wrong direction, which produces more negative thoughts. That could be an endless debate. If you learn to navigate your mental noise and work on getting your mind right, you can avoid spiraling down from feeling mildly depressed to severely depressed. The precursor to every action and emotion is a thought. In Alcoholic Anonymous, they use the term 'stinkin' thinkin' to describe the painful thoughts that compel you to drink to ease the pain.

Regardless of the circumstances, to become more mindful of your internal dialogue, handling it better, and learning to dismiss cognitive distortions must become your new way of life. Information and books like this one can certainly help and be a good additional resource.

There's got to be some middle ground between the two polar opposite mindsets of: 1) There is nothing I can do to help myself or no adjustments I need to make that are under my control— I have a diagnosis and need the right medication; and 2) It's all in my head, I'll just toughen up and be happier and think my way out of it. Medication or seeing someone for help? No way, I'm never doing that since that would mean I'm crazy.

Here is a good example from one of the readers of my monthly newsletter, Pam L, which sums this up well:

> All my life, I've been plagued with thoughts of every nature and description that ruled my life. I am, fortunately, very intelligent and well educated, yet powerless to free myself from these thoughts. I finally sought professional help and was immediately prescribed one of the selective serotonin reuptake inhibitors (Paxil). After taking this medication for about six weeks, I can finally read newsletters such as yours with clarity and insight and a desire to put such suggestions into action. Words pale when it comes to describing the joy I felt at FINALLY finding concrete methods to manage such wearisome and cumbersome thinking. Albeit, the medication

was a necessary first step, for it cleared the way and stilled enough thoughts to allow reason to enter.

This letter is a good reminder, even though it may be preferable to handle things without medications and their side effects, which may not be realistic for everyone. It's important to recognize that some people need additional help depending on the severity of the negative impact and life disruptions of the noise. There shouldn't be any shame in seeking that help and professional evaluation and treatment.

Here is one person's account with postpartum depression and the clinical trial for the recently approved drug to treat this:

> Stephanie, a mother of two from Connecticut, had no history of depression. But after giving birth to her daughters two years apart, she began crying nonstop, and lost interest in doing things she loved, like cooking and socializing. "I started having intrusive thoughts that would not go away," she recalled. "'Your daughter deserves a better mom, and your husband deserves a better wife.' That would just play on and repeat." Ultimately, she felt suicidal and feared she would harm herself if she stopped holding the baby. After her younger child's birth, she spent two weeks under round-the-clock suicide watch at home. The antidepressant she was prescribed, Zoloft, took three months, at increasing dosages, to eliminate her symptoms. Following the older child's

birth, Zoloft didn't help at all, so she volunteered for the brexanolone trial. Between 12 and 18 hours after the infusion started, "I actually woke up from a nap and those intrusive thoughts that played on repeat, they were gone," said Stephanie. After leaving the infusion site, "I felt like myself again. I wasn't 100 percent, but I was pretty close." She did not stop antidepressants altogether but switched to a low dose of Effexor.[11]

This is a scary story and another reminder that we need to regard mental health struggles with the same respect we give physical health struggles.

Medications do work well for many in reducing symptoms. They can take the edge off and cut through the resistance enough to allow therapy, the strategies in books like this, or other approaches to work. The pharmaceutical industry has developed many new drugs that weren't available back when most people with mental health conditions were treated on an inpatient basis, many of which were in horrible conditions in the old state hospitals.

In the SSRI class of drugs, I've heard that Lexapro has fewer side effects and works well for many. As always, it's better to consult with your physician. There may be new medications developed that work even better.

# 3. Can You Hear the Noise?

C an you hear the ever-present noise? Your brain is creating somewhere between 35 and 48 thoughts per minute. This chatty self-talk is happening right now as you are reading this. This is what the brain does. Neuroimaging studies suggest the normal resting state of the brain is a silent current of thoughts, images and memories that are not induced by sensory input or intentional reasoning but emerges spontaneously 'from within'. A Harvard University study concluded that nearly 47 percent of our waking hours are spent thinking about something other than what is actually happening.[12] You must recognize this so you can navigate all this noise. You can't navigate something that you're not aware of.

Our process of thinking is so internal that it's often easy to not be cognizant of it and recognize that we have a role in it. We wouldn't be surprised if we needed a drink of water after eating something spicy and we wouldn't be startled by the sound of our own voices since we know that we created these situations. More internally, it would be odd to consciously be aware of, and say to yourself, "Oh, I just blinked," or, "I just swallowed." Most of these functions go on in the background of our awareness. Now for the hardest one: How about feeling anxious, especially about a future situation? Can you tell the reason why you're feeling anxious is because of the anxiety-riddled thoughts you're thinking? Can you recognize those thoughts? That takes more insight and effort.

It causes us so much trouble to let our thought processes go on exclusively in the background, without noticing it or recognizing them for what they are— simply thoughts. I think it's unfortunate, for example, to be on your way home from work feeling upset and stressed, and just not having the self-awareness to recognize the noise that's going on in your head that's causing you to feel this way. Then you walk in the door and are not at your best, withdrawn, in a bad mood, not fun to be around, and not present with your loved ones. Anxiety can become manifested as irritability. Far too many people go through life this way.

What separates us from the rest of the animal kingdom is our brains are more developed, particularly the cerebral cortex area, and we have the conscious ability to be aware of what we're thinking. It's called metacognition, defined as the ability to think about what we think about. This empowers us to objectively analyze our thoughts to ensure they are serving our best interests.

Until I woke up to this, I never realized how negatively I thought about myself, other people, and life in general. I knew what I was worried about. I didn't know and wasn't grasping that it was my own thinking that was causing the feeling of being worried. I didn't know that the situation itself was neutral— neither good nor bad.

Some of the situations in my life were challenging. That's an unavoidable part of life, but it's a relative term since we all have different viewpoints on what's challenging.

But doesn't a substantial percent of our reactions and feelings emanate from our thoughts? Your thinking will always create the reality you are experiencing and perceiving. What percentage of your stress is self-created or self-inflicted? It's a lot more than people realize.

Some people have a tough time accepting this, and some don't want to hear it because this means they must assume some responsibility for what's going on. Some people ruminate about things that bother them and become experts in their problems, not in solving them, but in describing them in vivid detail to others.

It's easy to get entrenched in your positions and fall into a trap of complaining and justifying, which causes more complaining and justifying. This can become someone's normal reality and they get so used to thinking this way that it becomes their 'normal'. This is what is meant by automatic negative thoughts, or ANTs, and how they easily become automatic. When someone's in that pattern, if you ask them to examine their thinking and what they're dwelling on, or read a book like this, they may not only not want to hear it, but could accuse you of being judgmental. You ought to give yourself a pat on the back for being interested in information like this since it means that you're open minded and are willing to do some introspection and take action to help yourself.

In my old way of thinking, I followed the train of thoughts. This was counterproductive. I was reacting to mental activity but not realizing it was just mental activity— that I was producing it and had some control over it.

That was the opposite of mindfulness. Becoming aware and waking up to your thinking is just like waking up from a bad dream. We've all had the experience of being relieved after waking up and saying, "Thank goodness that was just a dream." This is the same thing, except you're awake and it's like a daydream. Both circumstances are about your brain creating things and how you're relating to these creations.

In the last few decades we've all heard much about mindfulness and its benefits, which is a great development. There have been many articles and research papers produced, studies funded, and apps created. It seems to be everywhere. My local high school had a recent mindfulness challenge for a month. Every morning from 7:00 to 7:05 a.m., people were encouraged, wherever you were, to be mindful for those five minutes.

Mindfulness can be defined many different ways. One is to consider it an ability— the basic human ability to be fully present and aware of where we are and what we're doing. Another is to consider it a practice— the effort of cultivating this awareness. Another is to consider it a way of thinking or quality of mind. The simplest definition is: to notice what you're noticing. In this moment. Being aware. Right here, right now. Noticing without judging or evaluating what you're noticing. Notice what you're noticing could be internal, external, or both.

First, there's external mindfulness. As an easy example, focus on taking a shower. Being mindful is to notice what it feels like to have the water spraying on you, taking in those sensations of the shower instead of having your attention diverted elsewhere, or pondering the upcoming day. Another example would be taking a walk outside and noticing all the details of what you're seeing in nature during the walk, instead of being elsewhere in your awareness or getting caught up inside of your head.

There is so much that you can do mindfully. You can wash dishes mindfully. If someone were to ask you what you're thinking about while mindfully washing the dishes, the answer should be, "Nothing. I'm just washing the dishes and totally focused on that." I've been told repeatedly that I can do better when eating more slowly and mindfully tasting, chewing and savoring the food. They even make forks nowadays that will prompt you when it's time to take your next bite by lighting up. This helps you learn to slow down and eat with more awareness.

I've been in mindfulness training sessions where everyone is handed a raisin. You are talked through several steps. First is to pick up the raisin and look closely at all the minute details of it— the folds and the wrinkles, etc. Then, feel the sensations on your fingers as you roll it around on them. Then you put the raisin in your mouth and become aware of how it feels in your teeth while chewing along with its taste, etc. If I started evaluating the raisin and comparing it to other raisins I've experienced, then I'm missing the point of the exercise.

Internal mindfulness is noticing the thoughts you're thinking. It doesn't mean judging or evaluating thoughts, because then you're reacting and no longer just noticing. Metacognition gives you the ability to consciously replace a train of thought that you don't want to entertain, let grow, or become a bigger deal in your mind. First comes the awareness.

At a Deepak Chopra seminar, he talked about awareness and did an exercise with the audience. He asked us to respond yes when he asked us the question, "Are you aware?" After a couple of repetitions, he said, "Now, don't respond until I raise my hand." It took a long time for Chopra to raise his hand; it seemed like forever. The intention was to notice more and be more aware in those moments while waiting. I wondered, "When will he raise his hand? Why isn't he raising his hand?" There was the noise, the dialogue, right there. It also made it easier to notice my breathing.

There are many examples of noise in popular culture that are revealing. In Mel Gibson's film, *What Women Want*, Gibson's character was able to hear all the thoughts that women around him were having, particularly Helen Hunt. He heard brutal honesty with no filter! Imagine if you had a transcript of all the thoughts that you thought in a day. There'd be hundreds of pages, with much you'd want to erase. You'd notice that we're continuously judging— ourselves, others, and our experiences.

Look to the Kevin Costner film, *For the Love of the Game*. As a pitcher in loud Yankee Stadium, Costner's character, Billy Chappell, can silence everything by saying to himself, "Clear the mechanism." Suddenly, it's so quiet he can hear only his breathing and the opponent in the batter's box becomes hyper focused visually; everything else is out of focus.

If only it were this easy in real life. There are several examples of mindfulness in the film which include him flashing back while on the mound as he visualizes when, as a boy, his father said to him, "Just calm down and throw the ball. Just play catch." Sports psychology emphasizes how what you say when you talk to yourself affects your performance.

Many music lyrics also mention the mental noise. In Lauren Daigle's song, *You Say*, she tells us:

> I keep fighting voices in my mind that
> say I'm not enough
> Every single lie that tells me I will
> never measure up
> Am I more than just the sum of every
> high and every low?

To become more mindful and self-aware of the constant dialogue inside our heads, one of the best things we can do is to notice how we're feeling. It's a great indicator of how we're thinking. A good prompt is, "What was going through my mind as I started to feel that way?"

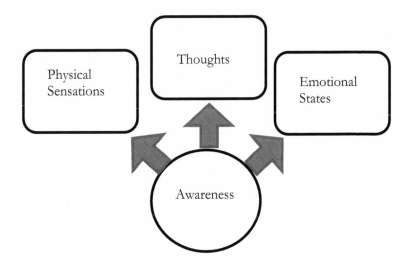

Also notice your breathing. You'll recognize it's shallow and rapid when you're feeling anxious or upset. When you notice that, you can just simply ask yourself, "Hey, what am I thinking about right now? Is this helping me or is this harming me?" When I say this, I don't mean the 50,000 thoughts, on average, we think daily. That would be exhausting and impossible. What's most important is to pay attention to what we're dwelling or ruminating on and causing emotions to stir up. You can notice that through your feelings, breathing and other bodily sensations, and periodically asking yourself the question. This can help you avoid a negative stress cycle as in the next page.

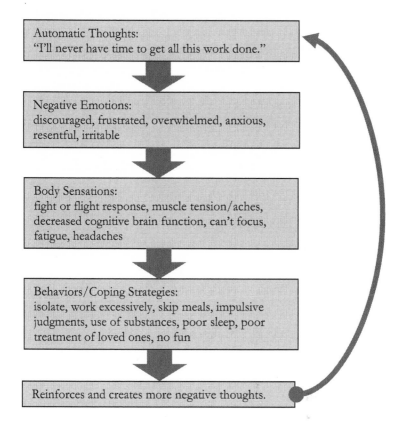

Automatic Thoughts:
"I'll never have time to get all this work done."

Negative Emotions:
discouraged, frustrated, overwhelmed, anxious, resentful, irritable

Body Sensations:
fight or flight response, muscle tension/aches, decreased cognitive brain function, can't focus, fatigue, headaches

Behaviors/Coping Strategies:
isolate, work excessively, skip meals, impulsive judgments, use of substances, poor sleep, poor treatment of loved ones, no fun

Reinforces and creates more negative thoughts.

For example, it's 11 p.m. and you feel like you should check your work email. Since the precursor for every action is a thought, mindfulness is being able to recognize the thoughts you're having about checking your email, and not just going ahead and doing it without awareness. It's being able to separate the thoughts from the action. Just because I think it, doesn't mean I have to do it. It's also being able to separate the thoughts from the feeling. Just because I think it, doesn't mean I have to feel it. I may think a stressful thought, but with mindfulness I don't have to entertain that thought and end up feeling stressed.

Meditation, described in chapters 9 and 10, helps you see the mental activity that you may have never noticed before. Some people describe their minds as a massive fast-moving highway, but meditation allows you to slow the traffic down so you can see individual automobiles. Without meditation, the brain can seem so chaotic that it feels like the cars are one huge line of steel.

It costs us so much to be a stress junkie, frantically rushing through life without awareness. Stress can be a physical, emotional, or chemical factor. But it causes bodily and mental tension and is a factor in disease causation. Stress is the perception of a physical or psychological threat, and the perception that one's resources are inadequate to deal with the threat. When you're threatened or stressed, or even when you're rushing through life trying to get it all done, biologically it's the same thing to your brain as rushing around to escape from a predator. That's the part of the brain that's active. Emotional responses are milliseconds faster than cognitive thinking responses. The brain defers to seniority and the older, more emotional parts of the brain take precedence when activated. The lightning-fast reactions that bypass the rational brain centers were useful survival responses from our past. The limbic brain system sends us the warning of a crisis and the body is alerted and is ready to act on our behalf. But since control has been shifted from the cerebral cortex to the limbic system, this effectively shuts off the cortex's ability for nuanced, innovative thinking and sophisticated analysis. You're still able to function, but just not very well. You usually don't know that the cortex is offline, but what you say and how you act is based on the fight-or-flight instinct and previous training.

This response was essential to get more blood flowing to our major muscles to help us outrun a predator. But no one can run fast enough to flee his own worries and thoughts. And do we really need more blood flow to our thigh muscles when we're reacting to a plethora of emails?

The first step is hearing it, noticing it, and being aware of it. As Jon Kabat-Zinn says, "The very first and most important step in breaking free from a lifetime of stress reactivity is to be mindful of what is actually happening while it is happening."

*used with permission    toothpastefordinner.com*

# 4. Why We Can't Rely on Our Brains

T here's a very sensical reason why our brains have a negativity bias, are much more interested in what could go wrong, and frankly, can be such a jerk to us. I had known that it was due to evolution, but it's not until you look more closely at the numbers and math that this makes sense. This can give you a paradigm shift and forever change the way you view your brain.

It's easy to forget that it's been roughly four million years since the earliest version of humankind began walking upright. They were called Hominids and had a brain one-third our size.[13] It's been a long and slow evolutionary process, and as we began using speech and more sophisticated tools, our brains have been evolving with us over a period of millions of years. It's only been 300,000 years since we began using fire.[14] Our current genetic modern human form, Homo sapiens, was getting a foothold around 50,000 years ago. The 50,000 years we've had this brain out of four million is not very long in the big picture. From an evolutionary perspective, it might be considered cutting edge, since it's only 1% of the total time.

During most of our stages of human cultural evolution, the rate of innovation and change was slow enough for genetic adaptation to keep pace. But in more recent times, the rate of change in our culture and technology has been lightning fast. One thousand years is a drop in the bucket from an evolutionary perspective. But from a human technological perspective? The progress that's been made in the last 500 years with the scientific revolution is incomparable. A big impetus for the scientific revolution was finally admitting what we didn't know and beginning a quest of discovery. Prior to this, most people felt everything that was important to know was already known by the elders and ancient texts.[15] Imagine if you lived in 500 BC and awoke from a deep slumber 500 years later, in 1 AD. Although there were advances, the world would look somewhat recognizable and basically the same. Likewise, if you awoke years 500 years later to 500 AD, 1000 AD, and 1500. But if you lived in 1500 and woke up in the year 2000 or today? Life wouldn't be recognizable. You'd think a smartphone, car, plane, skyscrapers and electricity would be from outer space. Our poor brains have not been able to adapt to all these advances in our external lives. They desperately need an update and a new operating system.

It's easy to forget what it was like 50,000 years ago when our current brains were formed. We can't begin to imagine what violence, physical danger, and stress disorder our species was exposed to— not only with vicious wild animals, but conflicts with other bands of humans over food or resources. In short, we either had lunch or were lunch.

Historians tell us we only began getting any semblance of

civilization 10,000 years ago. This was after the last ice age with the development of agriculture, which began to replace the hunter-gatherer way of life. This allowed for the growth of communities that were not nomadic. How civilized were conditions even 1,000 years ago? The threat of your village being surrounded during the night and attacked was omnipotent.

One could also argue that last century, the 20th century, was uncivilized in many parts of the world. Wars took a death toll of about 123 million. This breaks down to 37 million military deaths, 27 million collateral civilian deaths, 41 million victims of "democide" (genocide and other mass murder) and 18 million victims of non-democidal famine.[16]

We all should be grateful that we live today. Imagine trying to live without indoor plumbing, electricity, or automobiles? Those only became widespread about a little over 100 years ago. Imagine living without computers, the Internet, or cell phones? Or not ever knowing who was calling before picking up the phone?

What was the original prime directive of our brains? It was to keep us alive so our genes could be passed on. We forget that for 95% of the time we've had our current mental equipment, the threat of violent death was very high and life expectancy was very low. Keeping us safe from danger and issues of life and death was the brain's mission. To keep us alive, our brains needed to keep us on alert looking for threats. The quality of our lives or reducing anxiety was not, and is not, the primary concern of our brain. Take the question,

"Is there an enemy or tiger hiding behind that bush?" Your brain would rather have you assume yes and be wrong 100 times rather than assume no and be wrong once, which could be fatal. Take the carrot and stick analogy. Our brains are much more interested in the sticks. We can miss out on a carrot and there will be a chance for another carrot on another day. But miss and not be prepared for a dangerous stick coming our way? That means game over. No passing on of our genes.

We've got to grasp that even today, our brains are still operating this way. Always doing this job of searching for what is wrong or what could go wrong in our lives. When something went wrong back then, it usually meant life or death. Contemplating what's wrong or may go wrong was an essential. Now what our brains do is outdated, obsolete, and irrelevant (unless you live in war zone).

The parts of the brain that are largely responsible for the emotional, fear-based reactions, and the fight or flight response are the amygdala, a set of small, almond-shaped clusters of nuclei near the base of each hemisphere of the brain. They are part of the limbic system and are the opposite of the rational, logical part of the brain. They have other functions to which they contribute, as in processing the significance of stimuli related to other positive primal urges. Once, they kept us safe. Now they can make us go insane.

Since our brains haven't adapted, modern society has confused our amygdala into treating everyday financial woes, relationship issues, and career problems as real "life or death" situations. Today, the same pre-civilized stress and fight or flight reactions are triggered when we see we've received a message before even opening it, or we anticipate things not turning out well. Or, we ruminate on one negative or disappointing result from the day and overlook all the positive things that occurred.

Today's brains are irrational. Fifty awesome things may have occurred during your day, but what does your brain want to keep focusing on? That one setback. That's what's relevant to its threat analysis. The brain reminds you and re-plays your failures; every time it's replayed you feel the same emotions and responses that go along with it. In fact, as much as 77% of everything we think is negative, counterproductive, and works against us.[17]

Your brain is constantly scanning for danger and asking, "Is everything okay? Are you sure everything is okay? Well, what if _____ happens? You'd better be ready for that." This never stops. It's like a nervous squirrel scanning in all directions for predators while gathering acorns. It's trying to anticipate, trying to outsmart the danger. Being chill, calm and relaxed meant you were less likely to survive. This was as essential to the survival of our species as having a libido. The more anxious you were, the more likely you survived.

The brain also cannot process all the stimulation it's presented with. That is why we have unconscious bias. Unfortunately, what you're happy or grateful about is not as relevant to your brain since it's not relevant to its mission. That is dismissed and pushed aside so the brain can continue to scan for threats of what could, or is, going wrong.

The brain needs something to do, so this scanning is constant. It's like the newspaper— it must come up with something. There's not going to be a day with a blank newspaper with no news. Likewise, there will never be a time when your brain cannot not produce a compelling subject matter for you to get stressed and anxious over. This seems to happen frequently when we're trying to fall asleep. The brain wants to scan, review, and learn from situations that went, or almost went wrong during the day. Also, getting excluded from the hunter/gathering band was a death sentence since we need other people. Because of this, the brain also instinctually wants to scan about who we have wronged, who thinks we have wronged them, what people think of us and what is our social standing, so we don't get excluded.

Our brains can easily set off a chain reaction of panic when there's nothing to be anxious about. In today's world, it's not life or death. Reactions are rarely about physical danger or a physical stressor; it's mostly emotional stressors, things that we're either thinking about or how we're perceiving things.

While the cause of the response has changed, it's the same life or death response with the amygdala, reacting as though we're in danger and starting a chain reaction as cortisol, epinephrine and blood sugar rushes into the blood stream along with other harmful stress hormones, opening the door to a wide variety of mental and physical diseases.

Bad memories play a role here as your brain wants you to clearly remember when and how you've been in danger, to avoid it in the future. The more emotional it was, the more ingrained it becomes in the hippocampus and amygdala, which creates a larger emotional trigger and larger future reactions. We know that long-term environmental stress causes chemical changes in the brain. This can contribute to a chemical imbalance and an enlarged, hyper-sensitive and over reactive amygdala. However, with neuroplasticity that the brain is constantly changing and re-wiring, there is hope to calm this down.

We need to keep reminding ourselves that it's our brain, not us, that's creating these negatives from evolution and the outdated job it's still doing. This is tremendously helpful since you can eliminate the second guessing, ruminating, racing thoughts and wondering, "Why do I think this way? What's wrong with me?" You could even say, "I just have an over-active amygdala."

Gently remind yourself that your brain desperately needs a software update from the App Store. Since that's not forthcoming, tell yourself that you no longer need to be, or will be, ruled by life or death responses to things that simply are not life or death situations. You can thank your brain for trying to protect you. Tell yourself, "This is not life or death. This is not an emergency." When we do this, we no longer give it power over us.

Tell yourself that you've evolved past it; you've outgrown it. You're better than that. Your life is not an emergency. Since we become what we think about most of the time and our brains are constantly re-wiring, I've decided that I will stop being afraid of what could go wrong and will start being excited about what could go right.

# 5. Internal Fake News

Your brain discriminates negatively since it's doing its outdated and obsolete job of keeping you safe from physical danger. We must embrace that the default state of our brains is delusional. Your inner critic is a liar. It's not your fault and doesn't mean there is anything wrong with you or that you should have some sort of diagnosis. It's our brains that are delusional, not us.

The natural state of the brain is spontaneous wondering, mostly wondering or scanning for danger or things that could go wrong. Much of what the brain creates and enters our consciousness is not only negative but inaccurate. It's not factual or based in reality; it's fake. Our brain deceives us. It's convincing and presents things to us as if it's truth and important news. It appears like it's something that needs to be paid intention to, is urgent, and worthy of our attention. Look at the many news channels that have a banner on the screen: "breaking news". Does the banner ever come down? How can everything be breaking news? The purpose of the banner is to get and keep our attention, so we stay on their channel.

Internet sites are judged by advertisers by the number of clicks they receive on their headlines. They create 'click-bait' headlines that are designed to either frighten us, enrage us, or peak our curiosity. It doesn't matter to them, as long as we take the action they want by giving it attention and clicking on it.

Our brains do the same thing and can be very convincing with the thoughts it presents to us. Thoughts vie for our attention, as if they're saying, "Think me, think me," similar to the game Whac-A-Mole. Bad news sells because our brains, specifically our amygdala, are looking for something to fear. We can easily have anxiety that originates from thoughts in the brain's cortex and freak out about things that aren't even happening. It's almost like the amygdala is watching cortex television, similar to the Pixar's kid's movie *Inside Out*, and reacting to our various imaginations, many of which are about the past or future.

Some people are skeptical and dismiss what is presented to them by certain news media outlets, especially when it contradicts their beliefs. In 2016, just 32% of people told Gallup they thought the media reported the news "fully, accurately, and fairly." That number in late 2018 had risen to 45%. "Fake news" has become ubiquitous in our culture— a frustrating phrase for some, but nonetheless ubiquitous. Just because an article appears online doesn't mean it's accurate; you've got to find the original source as misinformation is frequently re-cited and snowballs.

Here's some breaking news: The garbage our brains report about us and our life is not a full, accurate, or fair picture! Internal, or self-created fake news is the worst kind of fake news. Because it's personal, about yourself, it's negative, and it's repetitive. The news cycle in the media only seems to last a few days; the headlines quickly move on to something else to get our attention. Too bad our internal news cycle is so much longer. We usually inundate ourselves with the same negative headlines about the same topics. "My life is a disaster", or "I'm such a loser" can be common headlines for some. It's called rumination in the psychology field and it's one of the most harmful things that sabotages our enjoyment and success in life. We've need to be skeptical, dismiss it, and keep it off the front page of our awareness. Put it on the back burner. Relegate it to the legal notice section.

The most effective way to do this, once we've increased our levels of awareness/mindfulness and are more adept at recognizing our mental activity, is to simply identify it as noise. Changing our relationship to it and how we view this noise, or internal fake news, is paramount. Although "ignore the noise" is a popular phrase, we can't ignore things that we view as important. The ideal is to see it as white noise that goes on in the background that we don't pay much attention to— as if we have a firewall between us and our noise.

Realistically, we need to work on creating a separation between our thoughts and ourselves to be able to grasp that you are not your thoughts, and your thoughts are not you. Your thoughts are just the result of the normal spontaneous wonderings of your brain. Here's my definition of what a thought is: brain secretions. I suppose we ought to be glad that we have them since otherwise we'd be brain dead. They are not a reflection of who you are or your character. In fact, a huge insight into the state of your mental health can be determined by where you fall in the graph on the next page.

A thought is just a thought. It has no power to grow or become a "thing" or anything else unless you give it that power by giving it your attention, focus, or energy.

The best technique to accomplish keeping thoughts at bay is "catch, label, and release". As soon as you recognize a harmful thought, simply say to yourself, "There's a thought." For example, it was somewhat shocking to me to think I'm now over 50. I had been having thoughts similar to, "You're over the hill now, too old; you should have accomplished more in life by now." That's complete garbage and fake news. Now I say to myself, "Well, there's a thought," and then release it by moving on to something else. You could have the thought (after business hours) that you ought to be checking your work messages. Many times, this is not the company's expectation and that's never been explicitly communicated. The goal is to recognize and catch that for what it is— another fleeting thought that the brain is trying to trick us with and get us to believe that we're in a state of emergency.

When I say, "There's a thought!" I attempt to do it with some joyful surprise, as if I'm playing a game and the more I catch the better I'm doing, like flashlight or laser tag. I'm glad that I caught it! I exposed it out of the dark. I exposed it for what it is. Thus, it can't be a concealed sniper firing at me and causing me stress. Those thoughts may return after I release them, then I'll probably catch them again. Every time I do this they fade even more. Those thoughts shrink, lose their emotional punch, become less scary, and less worthy of my time.

By saying, "There's a thought!" I can identify it and define it. By catching, defining and labeling those thoughts, they're diminished. Using a label to describe what's happening is especially effective. For example, instead of staying with the thought, "I'm a loser," say, "I'm having a thought that I'm a loser." Instead of giving power to the thought, "I'm going to blow this sale," say, "I'm having the thought that I'm going to blow this sale." It's a subtle difference, but it can help you gain the perspective that you are not your thoughts and your thoughts are not you.

We can't remind ourselves enough that a thought is just a thought. That's all it is. Nothing more, nothing less. They don't exist outside of our awareness. We forget that happy people have many of the same kind of negative thoughts as do depressed and anxious people. The only difference is in the relationship between the thoughts and the thinker: happy people are able to see their thoughts as thoughts and dismiss the ones they don't want. Our thoughts are not solid, like trees or objects that exist outside of us in some tangible way. Thoughts are like opinions. They should be taken with a grain of salt and looked at with healthy skepticism until proven true. There is nowhere else where the thoughts currently appearing to you are actually happening. Thoughts have no power to harm you unless you allow it. They come and they go. Just because my brain created it as part of its spontaneous wandering doesn't mean it's worthy of a second thought. I don't have to go there. Why should I? Most of the time it just makes me feel worse and doesn't help the situation.

When you've defined something as a thought you have a reset to choose if you're going to follow that train of thought any further. A train is another good analogy. Imagine how difficult it is to stop a train after it has momentum. With many of these trains of thought, don't argue or get pulled down that road since it's then more difficult to end that inner conversation. 'Cognitive entanglement' is the technical term of what we're looking to avoid.

Some people find it effective to actually thank their brain. If you're having anxious thoughts such as, "I hope this bus doesn't crash... I hope the driver knows what he's doing..." You can say, "Thank you, brain. Thank you for trying to keep me and my family safe. There's nothing that you really need to do right now. I've got it covered. I'm sorry you haven't been updated in thousands of years and you're still doing a stone-aged job, but I'm past that now." It's showing appreciation for its efforts, but also letting it know it can take a break.

Another effective technique to keep the noise at bay is to give it a name. Think of it has giving your inner critic, or the creator of your fake news, a name as if it's being voiced by another person or entity. This helps to get separation with your thoughts, discredit the noise, and see it as ridiculous. You can react with something similar to, "There you go again ___ ___, haven't we been over this before?"

Some people like to use the name of a person in their life whom they've found to be negative, offensive, abusive or used destructive criticism. This is especially damaging if it happened in childhood; the same type of critical voice you heard while growing up can easily get instilled and stay with you. Some people find it works to say something similar to, "That's just my *depression,* my *mother*, my *father*, my *fear*, or my *noise* talking." Remember when Franklin Roosevelt said, "We have nothing to fear but fear itself"? Let's revise that to, 'We have nothing to fear except fearful *thoughts*'. Thoughts cause the fear. To brush them aside by saying, "That's just my fear talking" can disarm the noise and its hold over you. It's a form of reframing, which is when the situation doesn't change, you just change the way you see it— but by doing that you transcend it.

You can also name the thoughts and noise by naming the story based on its subject matter. Often our thoughts are repetitive and involve the same stories about the same situations. For example, say one of your frequent stories is, "I'm going to run out of money." When thoughts appear like that you can say, "Oh, here's my *financial disaster* story again," and just wait and let it be until it goes away. It's a subtle difference, but it can give you needed perspective and detachment.

Some find it helpful to come up with a physical routine to

follow whenever you notice you've been triggered or getting off track. An example could be seeing a stop sign, stilling your body, and then inhaling and exhaling slowly a few times. It is preferable if you exhale longer than you inhale since that activates the parasympathetic, or rest and digest nervous system. Some people have had great success with the Emotional Freedom Technique, where you tap on the certain points of the body in a sequence. You also could come up with a specific phrase or visualization that you find soothing to employ while you're exhaling. This gives you a chance to stop and ask yourself what's happening. What are you reacting to? With this awareness, what's the best path forward?

It can also help to distract yourself by giving your cortex something to do and an alternative to think about. This gets that part of the brain on-line, so you can get out of the emotional limbic system of the brain. You could start to do some calculations, come up with a food or country that starts with each letter of the alphabet, or think about the contestants on a guilty pleasure reality TV show. A crossword puzzle or similar game can be an affective distraction. Certain types of music shift mental states and release dopamine. You can have a song from your past that you associate warm and happy memories with. Some people find tactile stimulation with a fidget toy or stress ball quiets the noise by giving the brain something else to focus on. Anything you can do to interrupt the pattern or cycle can be helpful.

For many years I said "cancel" when noticing a counter-productive thought. Then I realized that most of the time it's too adversarial and over the top. Saying "cancel" does help somewhat since it substitutes the initial thought with something else. I have met people who have had success wearing an elastic band on their wrist and snapping it when starting to get bothered by a particular train of thought. At times these more adversarial or dramatic resets or pattern interrupts can be helpful, but more often you'll get better results by being gentler.

One gentler technique is to calmly acknowledge the thought for a few seconds and then imagine it floating off and dissolving. Another would be to try noticing your thoughts as if they were leaves floating by in a stream. That means letting your worries flow over you, but don't respond to them, don't engage with; just let them be and then go. It's a way of being mindful about what you let into your brain. It's a "no big deal" attitude towards the negative thinking. This way your brain will stay calm. You're reinforcing that you know those thoughts are not real, so you take control. They are fleeting thoughts in your mind that are not a part of you. They come and go as they please.

These types of techniques are not a magic solution that will solve everything, but they help if you believe they can and give them a chance.

In fact, they've been proven to help. In one series of experiments, Jeffrey Schwartz, a research psychiatrist at the School of Medicine at the University of California at Los Angeles, found that incorporating practices like this can quiet activity in the circuit that underlies obsessive-compulsive disorder (OCD), just like medications do. When OCD patients were plagued by an obsessive thought, Schwartz instructed them to think, "My brain is generating another obsessive thought. Don't I know it's just some garbage thrown up from a faulty circuit?" After 10 weeks of this trial study, 12 out of 18 patients improved significantly. Before and after brain scans showed that activity in the orbital frontal cortex, the core of the OCD circuit, had fallen dramatically. Just like how medications effective against OCD affect the brain. Schwartz called it 'self-directed neuroplasticity', concluding that the "mind can change the brain."[18]

Treating your thoughts as garbage by physically throwing them in the trash has also been proven effective. Studies have proven that when people write down bad thoughts about themselves or their bodies and then throw the paper away, they less swayed by those doubts.

It's also powerful to use the fact that we dream as evidence of the craziness our brain creates. We've all woken up after an unsettling dream and said, "Thank God that was just a dream! I'm not in jail, I'm not stuck in a closet, I'm not paralyzed, or I'm not making a speech that I'm late and un-prepared for!"

Dreams seem vivid with the altered consciousness of your sleep cycle, but these scrambled and non-sensical dreams are just creations of your brain. They are part of the spontaneous wondering that's always happening. We forget this is the same thing that's happening while we're awake; just with not as much imagery, but a plethora of rumination.

So why not use the same response? This is an essential tool I use to navigate my noise. I say to myself, "Thank god that's just a thought." By saying this I'm putting my thoughts into a category. I'm not reacting to the content or subject matter of the thought. It's more detached. It's a great reminder that I am not my thoughts and my thoughts are not me. I don't have to believe them! I'm not responsible or a bad person just because a thought popped into my head. I didn't do anything to create it. There's no underlying motive or root cause I have to search for. Leave the dream analysis to Sigmund Freud.

Look at the tabloids with the latest celebrity gossip or scandal. It's not the truth. Every word is an exaggeration, taken out of context, and salacious. We usually don't believe much of it or think we need to take some action because of it.

The thoughts our brain produces create similar stories, and they often sound as dramatic as the tabloid articles. The problem is, we buy these stories and become fused or entangled with them. We don't step back to get a better perspective.

The problem isn't that we have negative and ridiculous thoughts. We all do. The problem comes when we believe our thoughts are true and pay them attention. They're mostly all garbage. We should treat them as garbage and dismiss them as fake news. They're not worthy of being on the front page of our lives. What makes it to the front page has to be vetted, fact-checked, or put on trial.

# 6. "I'm Done Thinking About You"

O ne of the best examples of mental toughness in action is from Gabriel Giffords, the former congresswoman from Arizona. She was shot at a public constituent event as a 9mm bullet fired point-blank at the left rear of her head passed through her brain and exited the left front of her head near her left eye. This devastating traumatic brain injury greatly altered the trajectory of her life, affected her speech, and forced her to resign from Congress to rehabilitate.

Jared Loughner, who shot her, was sentenced to life in prison without the possibility of parole. He killed a total of six people, to include a federal judge, and wounded 12 others in the incident.

At Jared Loughner's sentencing hearing, his surviving victims made victim impact statements. Both congresswoman Giffords and her husband, John Kelly, looked calmly at Loughner as he stood 20 feet away. Kelley spoke directly to Loughner, saying, "Mr. Loughner, you may have put a bullet through her head, but you haven't put a dent in her spirit and her commitment to make the world a better place. We want you to know that we are *done thinking about you.*"

That statement is so impactful. This is conjecture, but making an educated guess, they were essentially saying: 'You shot me in the head, but I will not be giving you any space inside of my head. You don't deserve it. I have too much life ahead of me. I choose to look forward, not backward. If I entertain thoughts about you and what happened, then you win and I'm accomplishing nothing but harming myself. The bottom line is, you're just not worth it.'

This is a great example for all of us to follow. We all have situations or people in our lives that we need to be done thinking about— for our health, our present and our future.

To be done thinking about something, first you must make a decision. The derivative of the word decision is to cut off from any other possibilities. Decide that you'll no longer be entertaining any thoughts or giving any energy to that toxic topic. This is the essence of mental toughness. Mental Toughness is another term that's frequently used but there's confusion as to what it means. When I'm speaking at a company or at a conference and I ask my audiences what it means to them, I usually get answers about preference and being able to survive through difficult times. But I'm asking specifically about *mental* toughness. Here is my definition of mental toughness, which I find simple and practical: you have the ability, and you've made it a habit, to not allow your mind to go down roads where you don't want it to go. A mentally tough person exercises this ability frequently and it becomes second nature. Mental toughness is also understanding and adhering to the old phrase, "The mind makes a wonderful servant but

a terrible master." I think a better way of saying that would be, "The *brain* makes a wonderful servant but a terrible master."

I wouldn't use the words "mentally weak", but some people are tortured by their own thoughts. They allow their minds to pull them in multiple directions, to their own detriment. Mental Toughness is having the awareness, focus and commitment to say to yourself, "No, I'm not going there. That's a slippery slope. It's a cesspool of negativity that I refuse to immerse myself in. It's just going to create emotional states that are not going to serve me."

A helpful concept in being mentally tough, navigating the noise and keeping your mind right is to consider the brain and the mind as two separate entities. The brain creates all these random thoughts as part of its natural and normal spontaneous wondering, but your mind is different. Your mind, with its metacognition— the ability to think what we think about— is the director that decides what will play on the stage of your consciousness. The mentally tough use their minds to keep their brains in check, to keep its noise in the background, and dismiss it as unworthy of its attention. Their minds are adept at being very selective to which of the 50,000 or so thoughts the brain creates on a daily basis will be entertained and allowed a place on its stage. I've seen T-shirts with the phrase, "Think good thoughts" on them. In reality, that's exhausting and impossible. A better saying would be, "entertain good thoughts", but it's probably not catchy enough for a T-shirt.

When Congresswoman Giffords said she was done thinking about the man who shot her, that doesn't mean no thoughts about him would enter her mind, just that she would dismiss them, wouldn't entertain them, or allow them to fester.

We forget that we can dismiss just about any thought at any time. Just because we think it doesn't mean we have to analyze it, or that it's a legitimate "thing" that we need to deal with in our lives.

You could be sitting in a movie theater, intending to take a break from the usual concerns of life, and the following thoughts arise: "What color should I paint the family room? It's in such bad shape and is so embarrassing. When am I ever going to get to it? I'm such a procrastinator." Most people could recognize that it's far from impossible or arduous to say, "No, not now, time to bring my attention back to this movie and enjoy it." How often do you think about getting hit by lightning? What would you do if you started thinking about that? I think for most of us we can easily dismiss those thoughts.

A more difficult example is when our oldest child, Olivia, turned eight and was diagnosed with type 1, or juvenile diabetes. It's an autoimmune disease where our antibodies that fight off infection attack the beta cells in the pancreas that create insulin. It's not completely known why this happens, but you become insulin-dependent. The medical community is getting closer to either a cure, or some way of enveloping or protecting the beta cells so you only need one treatment a year, or a type of artificial pancreas to lessen this exhaustive monitoring. In the meantime, diabetes is a chronic, relentless disease. You must constantly monitor blood sugar— how many carbs you're eating, and how many units of insulin you need to compensate for those carbs. We're fortunate that Olivia is so responsible in managing it with an ever-increasing independence.

But what about our two younger boys? Will they develop diabetes? They passed the eight-year threshold, but that doesn't mean they can't get diabetes later in life. If one child develops diabetes it doesn't mean the other siblings will as well. There are families with more than one child and families with just one child afflicted. Whenever my wife and I begin to think about our sons being diabetic and what that would be like, we both agree that we just can't go there, won't go there. That's not a train of thought we'd want to allow to leave the train station. It wouldn't get us anywhere. That wouldn't help us or accomplish anything. We dismiss it.

It's helpful to incorporate the mental law of substitution. This states that only one thought at a time can be held by your conscious mind. It seems as if we think many thoughts simultaneously; our thoughts shift rapidly and the "subject" changes quickly. If the process was slowed down, you'd see that it's just one thought at a time. As soon as that initial thought, perhaps the initial unsettling thought, is replaced by a different thought, that initial thought is gone. You're no longer thinking it. That's just how the brain works. You can't hold more than one thought at a time. Also, you can't *not* think about something. You've got to think of something else to interrupt the pattern and change the discourse.

For the next minute, try not to think about pink elephants. It's impossible. You can, however, think of blue elephants. Now the thought about pink elephants has been replaced. When you use the catch, label, and release technique from the previous chapter, just saying, "There's a thought!" replaces the initial one. Whenever I start to project negatively into the future and the things that could go wrong, I replace thoughts and release them by moving on to something else.

You sometimes see in media interviews where the person being asked a question doesn't want to answer it or give any energy. They will bluntly say, "Next question." We can say to ourselves, "Next thought." This is mental toughness in action.

This is something we can do, and we get better with practice. We can find inspiration in the stories of people being mentally tough in situations more challenging than our own; like Gabby Gifford's. I found several more of these in a book by Nancy Koehn, *Forged in Crises— the power of courageous leadership in turbulent times*. In it, she profiles five leaders faced with tremendous obstacles. Ernest Shackleton and his crew were marooned on an Antarctic ice floe in early 1915. It took almost two years for his entire crew to be rescued— miraculously without the loss of any life. Imagine the mental toughness that took— not only for him to keep his own mind strong but to project it to his crew since they looked towards him for strength. Personally, I can't stand the cold and would have really struggled in that environment.

Major health crises can affect anyone. Cancer survivors continually amaze me. It must take such mental strength to keep your thoughts on health, recovery, your blessings, and not the disease. I was moved by Andy Whitfield, the actor who played the lead role in the Starz TV series *Spartacus*, who died at the age of 39, eighteen months after being diagnosed with non-Hodgkin's lymphoma. He left a wife and two young children, and his fight with the disease and eventual succumbing to it was filmed in a documentary entitled, *Be Here Now: the Andy Whitfield Story*, as it follows him on his dramatic journey to cure himself. Both Andy and his wife had matching tattoos done on their forearms with that phrase, 'Be Here Now', to affirm that they were taking Andy's healing into their own hands and living life fully in the present moment, not in the shadows of the disease. Watching the documentary reminded me that you just never know what's going to happen in life. Andy was someone who appeared to be the epitome of health, but just quickly faded away. It also reminded me that I have no problems. No real problems, anyway; if I don't, my mind doesn't allow my brain to convince me that I do.

People at some point get tired of all the negative thinking and ask themselves, "Why do I think this way or say these things to myself?" Perhaps they realize, "I don't have to think this way; it's not a requirement. It's been a habit and something I've gotten used to. But I'm not going to think this way anymore." How liberating this is! After all, if you're not in charge of your own thinking, then who or what is? You can say to yourself, "Enough already. It's time to stop this. There's no reason for this. Ruminating doesn't help or solve any problems." I love the phrase, "Worrying does not empty tomorrow of it troubles. It empties today of its strength."

Remind yourself that not everybody who is in your situation or shares your circumstances will think the way you do. Everyone thinks differently. We all have the same physical world, but we all have our private internal worlds with separate theaters playing different shows. Some of these private dialogues are very dramatic. Sometimes when I'm on a plane, I wonder how many of the 150 passengers have thoughts about the plane crashing. I wouldn't expect there would be many, but there are probably a few on each flight. The reality is you're more likely to get hurt driving to the airport.

Someone who's in his early 20's may lament the loss of his youth and teenage years. On the other hand, I play Ultimate Frisbee with a few people in their mid-60's who go all-out diving for discs, have more skill than many younger players, and don't appear to show their age. I asked one of the sixty-five-year-olds I play with if he thinks much about his age or getting older and he told me, "I can't control it, so no, I don't think that way."

What thoughts we give attention to is voluntary and can be controlled. We never know how strong we are until there's nothing else left to do but to be strong.

A great exercise is to write down any situations or people in your life to whom you'd like to declare you are done thinking about and want to give less of your energy and space in your head to. I'll bet most of these external situations we face haven't literally invaded our heads as what happened to Gabby Gifford's.

# 7. Turn Up the Volume on the Noise

Sometimes our efforts at mindfulness, being aware of our dialogue, and the catch-and-release technique aren't working effectively. We can become so acclimated to our noise, broadcasting the same lies and fake news at the same frequency, that it becomes all we know. We can't see the forest for the trees. The noise can be stealthy or camouflaged, like a sniper hiding in the brush, lobbing hurtful statements to us.

Our inner critic can become embedded in us in childhood, transferred from a parent or influential figure, and we just unconsciously accept its presence— like white noise, but an evil one. This is what is meant by automatic negative thoughts, or ANTs, and how they can easily become automatic. Some of these lies and harmful thoughts can be looping around in our heads for a very long time. This is when we must turn up the volume on the noise or navigate right into it to hear it more clearly. We need to modify what's normal and see our harmful noise as abnormal— like a cancer that no longer belongs there.

There have been many times when I felt anxious, negative or down and I've had to forcefully ask myself, "Wait a minute, what am I saying to myself right now?"

In other words, what's the problem? Is there really a problem? Or, is it just the baseless thoughts I'm thinking about? These thoughts I'm having, are they old programming from way back when that I don't need anymore? How embedded are these thoughts? We are generally hardest on ourselves and say things to ourselves that we'd probably never allow anyone else to say. There's a lot of labeling, which is when we call ourselves a global name, which generally goes on. We've all seen times when somebody will say something obnoxious and the other party will respond with, "Excuse me?" That's what you must do internally with your own dialogue. Getting ahold of that volume control and turning it up allows you to recognize and expose it for what it is and get it out of its camouflage.

Shad Helmsetter has a great book entitled *What to Say When You Talk to yourself.* I love that title. This book has been out for a long time and I've found it helpful. However, some of us may need something closer to *Can I Hear What I'm Saying to Myself?*

What is it that you're thinking? As I wrote in the mindfulness chapter, your breathing is a good indicator of when things are off. Getting in tune with how you're feeling is helpful since it's our thinking that creates our emotional states.

If you're struggling with this, a simple exercise that helps many is to draw a picture of a stick figure representing yourself. You could draw it with a certain emotion depicted on the face if you'd like. Then draw some thought bubbles above the head of your stick figure and write in why the stick figure feels the way it does. What you write down will usually be a hint about what's bothering you. Then you expand it to write down what it is you're thinking about or saying to yourself.

Reducing the noise to writing is one of the best things you can do. Our head is not a great place to organize, adjudicate, get clear on, or challenge our thinking. Writing it out on paper, on a keyboard, dictating it, or keeping a journal are techniques that can work. It helps you to get rid of the feeling of bouncing all around inside of your head. Far too many of us ruminate way too much. We overthink and over explain things. Frequently it's about the same types of situations and it seldom stops.

It's rare, but so helpful to say to oneself, "Let me just take a little time to write this down so I can get clear on what is going on in my head." We've all struggled to fall asleep with lots on the mind, then you finally take the action to write out a list and get a sense of relief from it. Seeing it in writing is eye-opening. You may react with something similar to, "No wonder why I've been feeling so anxious, depressed or miserable— look what I say to myself!" We frequently jump to conclusions in life, but don't recognize the jumps we've made until we write it out.

Writing has also been proven to be good for your health. In a control group study, a blood test was taken from a group who were asked to begin journaling for 20 minutes at the end of their day for two weeks. The journal could be anything about their life— what they're glad about, mad about, anxious about, etc. At the end of the time period a second blood test was taken, and the group that was journaling had an enhanced white blood cell response compared to the control group. Writing allows you to express how you're feeling without fear of being judged. If you're upset with someone, a great way to dissipate your emotions and noise is to write the person a letter that you don't intend to send.

Why not try writing it out? Yes, it's probably new and different for you. It might seem like a strange thing to do at first. The great Thomas Jefferson quote, "If you want something you have never had, you must be willing to do something you have never done," applies here. If you haven't been able to effectively navigate your mental noise to this point, this writing technique may just be that thing you've never done that will get you the peace of mind that's been elusive.

Writing also helps us to get real literal and be able to refute the blanket statements and ANTs that we say to ourselves, many of which are outrageously self-deprecating. The garbage that we say to ourselves is so toxic. They're things we'd never allow anyone to say to our kids.

What frequently happens is we start to snowball on something. We think one thought, which causes another, and another. If you don't catch it, it's the mental equivalent of getting stuck in the mud as your tires go deeper into a rut, or how a snowball grows as it rolls down a hill. The brain's thoughts are very deceptive and convincing, and before you know it you've reached a conclusion, which most of the time is premature, incorrect or irrational.

You can have a mental snowball about anything. For example,

a thought can pop into your head that you may have a financial crisis if a few situations happen a certain way; you can then leap to planning your new life in a homeless shelter.

A seminar participant once told us about one of her most common mental snowballs. This revolved around her husband, who plays in a bowling league every Wednesday night. He frequently arrives home later than he's supposed to. As you read this snowball, keep in mind this all happens very quickly, all within seconds.

Here are the thoughts in order that popped into her consciousness after she looked at her watch and realized he was late again:

- "He's 45 minutes late again."

- "How could he do this to me again?"

- "Doesn't he love me anymore?"

- "I don't deserve to be treated like this anymore."

- "We should go back into counseling."

- "We're probably a hopeless cause and should just end things now."

- "I know I should have married that other guy I was dating in high school."

- "I bet he's with that lady down the street."

- "I ought to wait outside her house to see if they come back together."

- "I wonder if there's any way to track his phone to get his location."

- "I wonder if this is a no-fault divorce state, or if I get more than equal martial assets if I can prove infidelity."

- "Well, I hope nothing happened to him."

- "Nothing had better have happened to him."

- "I don't know what I'd do without him."

- "Maybe I should start calling the local emergency rooms."

- "The police are probably going to knock on our door any minute, and I'm going to get some awful news."

- "Look at this place. This house is in no shape for a funeral."

See how that can build, how that can grow? This may seem ridiculous to you, but it's more common than many of us realize. It's just part of the human condition.

Here's another one that a reader sent me that she found online, posted anonymously. It is a wife's diary entry:

"Tonight, I thought my husband was acting weird. We made plans to meet at a nice restaurant for dinner. I was shopping with my friends all day long, so I thought he was upset about the fact that I was kind of late, but he made no comment on it. Conversation wasn't flowing, so I suggested we go somewhere quiet, so we could talk. He agreed, but he didn't say much. I asked him what was wrong: he said, "Nothing." I asked him if it was my fault that he was upset. He said he wasn't upset, that it had nothing to do with me, and not to worry about it. On the way home, I told him that I loved him. He smiled slightly and kept driving. I can't explain his behavior and I don't know why he didn't say, 'I love you too.'

When we got home, I felt as if I'd lost him completely, as if he wanted nothing to do with me anymore. He just sat there quietly, watching television. He continued to seem distant and absent. Finally, with silence all around us, I decided to go to bed. About 15 minutes later, he came to bed. But I still felt that he was distracted, and his thoughts were somewhere else. He fell asleep; I cried. I didn't know what to do. I'm almost sure that his thoughts were on someone else. My life is a disaster."

Here is the husband's diary entry for the same day:

"Motorcycle wouldn't start today... can't figure out why."

Such dichotomies are not uncommon. We all have private melodramas that play out in our heads that people around us aren't aware of. The above two anecdotes were from women, but this is not stereotypical; men have the same dynamics going on.

Many of these mental snowballs are repetitive and aren't properly resolved. Many of the thoughts we're having today we had yesterday; and many of the thoughts we're having today we'll have tomorrow.

To get clear on how this process happens, it's a great exercise to stop reading and write about one specific thing that you've recently been feeling anxious, stressed, or upset about. Begin with the initial thought. Next, list all the other thoughts that grow from that first one. Keep extending your thought to an outrageous degree, which is known as awfulizing.

You should gain some insight into the patterns of your thinking.

Another exercise which may expose some silent or hidden assumptions and irrational beliefs is called the downward arrow technique. Often, as the process continues, you will either arrive at a clearly absurd irrational thought or uncover a real issue that needs to be dealt with.  In any case, the information is useful. Begin by writing down a thought about a situation that's causing you discomfort. Then answer the same question about that thought and for each subsequent new thought. A good question is, "If that were true, why would it be upsetting to me? What would it mean to me?"

For example, you could start with the following thought: "I'm not appreciated and valued at my company."

"If that is true, why would I be upset? What would that mean to me?"

↓

---

"If that is true, why would I be upset? What would that mean to me?"

↓

---

You just keep going with this until you make a discovery. It might be a long-held erroneous core belief that it's time to move past. Many times it's about how we see ourselves, the world, or other people.

By turning up the volume on the noise, the objective is to discredit it. We can discover our thinking patterns and which ways our thinking is distorted. We all have distorted thinking and our brains are skewered to create internal fake news that seems real. There are some common forms of distorted thinking and deceptive traps you can get hooked into. To learn which ones you get entangled with is great self-awareness and gives you a powerful weapon to discredit the noise. Here are some of the most common. These are adapted from Dr. David Burn's book, *The Feeling Good Handbook*.:

- Discounting the positive— For whatever lame reason you come up with, the positive, good things and accomplishments in your life don't count. It's as if they somehow don't apply to you, or you're viewing it as if you had nothing to do with it, almost like an imposter created the accomplishment, therefore not giving yourself any credit. The imposter syndrome is deceptive. Our brains naturally immerse in this distortion since it's biased towards the negative, so we've got to recognize this and work at balancing it out.

- Emotional reasoning— You think that things are the way you feel about them. You forget that everyone's entitled to their own viewpoints, but not their own facts. Just because you see a situation as screwed up, that doesn't make it a fact that it actually is screwed up. It also doesn't mean that everyone else would see it the same way. Some people would view it as wonderful. Helpful phrases to remember are, "To each their own," and, "One person's garbage is another person's treasure." Many times, it's the lens we view things through that colors everything, since we see things not as they actually are, but how we are. Our reality is colored much more on our past experiences than by what is actually happening to us in this moment.

- Mind Reading— You assume you know what other people are thinking. You put imaginary judgmental thoughts in other people's heads, that you fervently believe, which makes you feel insecure. You conclude that other people are looking down on you, are angry, or disappointed in you. You interpret people's actions, or lack of, to mean the worst and spell gloom and doom. Most of the time you haven't asked any questions, no one has explicitly told you anything, you don't have all the evidence or facts, but regardless of all this, you're so sure of yourself and set in your thinking.

- Labeling and comparing— This is the most common way we beat ourselves up. We call ourselves global names such as, "I'm a jerk; I'm stupid; I'm an awful parent or spouse." Instead of seeing setbacks as inevitable mistakes and learning opportunities that are part of living, we make global criticisms to ourselves about who we are. What we say to ourselves tends to be outrageously unfair. They're things we'd never allow anyone else to get away with saying to us or to our kids. Most of us realize that we are our own worst critic. We need to generalize our successes more often and minimize our failures. Comparing yourself to others is always a no-win proposition since you can always find someone who you think is better at various aspects of life. I've noticed this type of noise in myself when I'm at the

CrossFit gym I recently joined. I must ignore it and focus on encouraging myself and not the people around me, most of whom are better athletes and can do all kinds of difficult movements with their bodies. It's unclear who came up with the following quote but it's one of my favorites, "Don't compare your beginning to someone else's middle."

- Control delusions— There are lots of control freaks in this world. Do you know any? This distortion could mean that you take on feeling guilty and responsible for things that are really not your responsibility or under your power. There's a reason why many 12-step groups advocate admitting powerlessness. The pressure of having superhuman powers and orchestrating life according to your wishes is off. You admit that you're powerless over many things to stop you from feeling crazy that it's your fault or responsibility. This and that. We don't have control over most things in life, especially other people. This distortion can also mean you view things as though you have zero control and responsibility, a helpless victim. My favorite phrase about control is, "I finally got a grip when I learned to let go."

- Jumping to conclusions— Without sufficient credible evidence, you predict things will turn out badly. This is also known as fortune telling. We need to remind ourselves that we don't have all the facts and information. There's no harm in being prepared for challenges, but when you draw premature conclusions, you overestimate threats and underestimate opportunities; that is when it becomes harmful. Things may not turn out the way you'd like; things may also turn out better than you ever could have imagined! Which assumption is better for your health and success in life? If you work in sales, don't take silence or a non-answer for a 'no' answer.

- Overgeneralizing— You see one negative event as an infinite pattern of defeat, from which there is no escape or end. You use words like "always", "never", "all", "all the time", "every", "everyone" and "every time" too often, as "This always happens to me," or "All men or women are blank." This really happens frequently, often, sometimes, or rarely, but not always. It's not an absolute black or white. For example, the entire day or the entire weekend was not a disaster, there had to be some good in there.

- Self-limiting beliefs— You use confirmation bias to find the evidence to back up your beliefs and reject any opposing evidence. This prevents you from trying new things, taking risks, and reaching your full potential. People pick up on this and how you describe yourself. It's more difficult for us to see this ourselves. We use phrases like, "I couldn't," or "That won't work." There's too much information around us for our brains to process at any one time. We all have biases, many of which are unconscious. A belief is simply a set of thoughts that we've been attached to for a long time and not objectively questioning. Technology is making confirmation bias worse. You've probably noticed that, after you search or shop for an item online, you keep getting ads for that item presented to you. Or, if you click on a certain type of article, more of the same type of article appears in your news feed, making it seem more newsworthy and legitimate.

- <u>All or nothing thinking</u>— If a situation falls short of your expectations of perfection, you see it as a total failure. Perfectionism causes much heartache. Many people put pressure on themselves to be perfect, which is an illusion. Some things are going to go wrong. Just because one thing goes wrong doesn't mean the entire situation is a total loss. If I leave something out of a speech that I meant to include, that doesn't mean the speech was a failure. A few people may not like it, but that's okay and to be expected, and I don't need to obsess on it.

- <u>Personalization</u>— You think everything somehow has something to do with you. Self-absorption and narcissism seem to be more prevalent these days. Some of us need to work on getting over ourselves. If you think all roads lead back to you and you take everything personally, that's an exhausting way to live. We need to remind ourselves that we're not the center. If we weren't in the picture, most things would proceed just fine. The acronym QTIP, for quit taking it personally, is a good reminder.

- <u>Self-blame</u>— You blame yourself for things that are not solely your fault, under your control, or your responsibility. Guilt is feeling bad about an action or decision you made. Shame is feeling bad about how you are as a person. It's the difference between saying, "I screwed up and learned from it, and, I'm a screw-up." This has a devastating impact on our self-esteem. The healthiest mindset is to understand there is a contribution percentage and you may have contributed to a challenging situation, but it wasn't all you. This is especially hard for the people we care about and for parents, since other people are going to do what they're going to do and are responsible for their own choices. Other people have their shortcomings and may not have the capacity to meet our needs or be the way we'd like them to be, but that's not our fault or a reflection on us. Having a loved one who is an addict is heartbreaking; but blaming yourself for his/her addiction just compounds the heartbreak.

- Mental filtering— You pick out one negative detail about something and focus on it to the extent that you don't see anything else or any of the positives associated with the situation. This is easy to do with other people by focusing on a trait that annoys you but not seeing the larger picture of the person's positive qualities. It's also easy to do with ourselves by discarding, dismissing, or not acknowledging our strengths.

This list can give you powerful insights by identifying your most common patterns of distorted thoughts. Reviewing this list can be a sudden wake-up call that causes you to declare, "That's exactly what I've been doing to myself and it ends today!" Recognizing the pattern may be all you need to stop the snowball from recurring. This is exciting since distorted thinking is toxic and life is too short to keep going down the same path.

I'm continually amazed by the wide-ranging diversity of how people think and their thought patterns. Everyone has different experiences, viewpoints and perspectives. It's sad to see how some people think. No wonder why they feel anxious or depressed. Garbage in, garbage out. A healthy perspective with others could be something like the following: "It's so interesting that you think that way, that you see it that way. That's so different than how I think about it." This can get deeper as our belief systems are also wide-ranging, and whatever people believe is true for them and makes perfect sense to them. Good luck trying to get someone to change his/her beliefs. However, you may have some luck getting people to recognize their distorted thinking, which leads to erroneous beliefs, especially self-limiting beliefs.

To delve further into this topic, some good self-assessments that you can easily search for online, and download PDFs and scoring guides, are the Dysfunctional Attitudes Scale, or DAS, and the Automatic Thoughts Questionnaire, or ATQ.

# 8. Navigate Into the Noise to Challenge it

T he next step to changing our thoughts and noise is to tell ourselves how and why the fake news that our brain creates is fake news. The latest promotional tag line for *The New Yorker* magazine is: *"Fighting Fake Stories With Real Ones."* That is exactly what we have to do with our internal stories— become an investigative reporter or a detective and impartially investigate the legitimacy of our internal fake news. We need to examine what we wrote on the writing exercise in the last chapter and speak up, talk back, and poke holes in that logic. We need to tell ourselves how and why it's inaccurate. We need counter-arguments, as though we're in a debate. It really is a debate between the unhealthy, irrational and dysfunctional part of ourselves and the healthy, functional and rational part.

This practice is the essence of Cognitive Behavioral Therapy (usually referred to as CBT), which is based upon the idea that how you think determines how you feel and behave. It's also based on the idea that problems aren't caused by situations themselves, but by how we interpret them in our thoughts. This can then affect our feelings and actions. In the 1960's, people who suffered from anxiety would have been advised, taking a cue from Freud, that they need to uncover the unconscious forces driving their fears. By the 70's, a more practical approach had taken hold: Learn to change the thoughts and behaviors that lead to anxiety. CBT teaches you to view your own thoughts differently. For example, to see a failed date not as proof that you'll never be loved, but as a minor event that didn't work out. Therapists coach you to challenge and change what you think; typically you're given homework. This involves keeping a record of the negative thoughts you've had, and what a more rational alternative could be to each thought, along with how this made you feel. The goal is to understand how your thoughts impact your life in significant ways, and to become aware of your irrational thoughts so you will naturally learn to change them.

On the rare occasions when we can't find any inaccuracies or distortions, we must tell ourselves that thinking like this is toxic and just makes things worse than they already are. The bottom line is, when we get upset by the things we say to ourselves, we need to say something different. We need to say something that takes the power away of the mental snowball, so it melts and doesn't reoccur. If you think about it, getting yourself upset by your own thoughts is like writing yourself a nasty email then forwarding it to others and complaining about it!

When your emotions are running high, it's harder to do this. You need to let things diffuse before you try to put a logical spin on your distorted thinking. It's important at some point to stop and write out a response to your mental snowball, clearly delineating your reasoning and arguments. The list of the most common cognitive distortions and identifying the ones that catch you should provide plenty of ammunition to deflate distorted thoughts.

Here are some more tools and techniques, or effective retorts, you can use to challenge and discredit your noise, and do some cognitive restructuring:

### Maybe, maybe not

This has saved me a lot of heartache over the years. It reminds me that I don't know for certain. Perhaps someone is disappointed with me; maybe they're not. Maybe that situation will happen; maybe it won't. Maybe it will rain at an important upcoming outdoor event, maybe not. Maybe my two younger children will contract type 1 diabetes; maybe they won't. That's a good mantra to keep repeating to ourselves. This helps to alleviate the thought distortions of mind reading and jumping to conclusions.

Music and song lyrics can be a soothing reminder and another tool to help us with our mental toughness. In Bebe Rexha's song *Meant to Be,* she tells us:

> If it's meant to be, it'll be, it'll be
> Baby, just let it be
> If it's meant to be, it'll be, it'll be
> Baby, just let it be

There are so many examples in music, and you can easily find a few songs that can help keep you grounded. Having a particular song stuck in your head may be better than the alternative of a negative loop. Some people even assign a designated 'recovery' song that lifts them up when feeling low. Paul Simon said it well in *50 Ways to Leave Your Lover:* "The problem is all inside your head she said to me. The answer is easy if you take it logically." Too many of us create problems in our heads due to a lack of incorporating logic into our thinking.

There are just so many unknowns and uncertainties in life. We have to do a better job at being okay with that. It doesn't do anyone any good to torture ourselves and get so wound up and anxious over it. "I just don't know." Be okay with that statement and comfortable not knowing.

A helpful reminder is the old parable of the Chinese farmer:

A farmer and his son had a beloved stallion who helped the family earn a living. One day, the horse ran away, and their neighbors exclaimed, "Your horse ran away, what terrible luck!" The farmer replied, "Maybe so, maybe not. We'll see."

A few days later, the horse returned home, leading a few wild mares back to the farm as well. The neighbors shouted out, "Your horse has returned, and brought several horses home with him. What great luck!" The farmer replied, "Maybe so, maybe not. We'll see."

Later that week, the farmer's son was trying to break one of the mares and she threw him to the ground, breaking his leg. The villagers cried, "Your son broke his leg, what terrible luck!" The farmer replied, "Maybe so, maybe not. We'll see."

A few weeks later, soldiers from the national army marched through town, recruiting all the able-bodied boys for the army. They did not take the farmer's son, still recovering from his injury. Friends shouted, "Your boy is spared, what tremendous luck!" To which the farmer replied, "Maybe so, maybe not. We'll see."

The lesson of the story is, we don't know what is going to happen; we just think we do. We often make a big deal out of nothing and create all kinds of wild scenarios. Most of the time we are wrong.

## What evidence do I have and how do I know for sure?

These two work better in tandem since they feed off each other to deescalate. Imagine a helpful friend trying to assist his buddy challenge his thinking when reacting to erroneous conclusions. It could go something similar to the following:

Helper: "Well, I hear you, but what evidence do you have?"

Friend: I just know.

Helper: But how do you know for sure?

Friend: Well, I just know.

Helper: But what evidence do you have?

Friend: Well, I just know.

Helper: But how do you know for sure?

This could go on for a while. This type of thought questioning may result with them concluding they don't know for sure, need to dial back their reactions about rash conclusions, and help reach the conclusion that there are a lot of unknowns and uncertainties in life.

## Put that thought on trial

Closely related to the last strategy is putting that thought or line of thinking on trial. Think of a witness on the stand and how an attorney will try and introduce doubt, as in, "How do you know for sure it was my client that you saw at the crime scene?" Courtroom trials have strict rules. Verdicts are rendered by a preponderance of the evidence or by beyond a reasonable doubt. There are also rules of evidence, which encompasses the rules and legal principles that govern the proof of facts in legal proceedings. They must be authenticated and verified. What doesn't count as evidence are your gut feelings.

This is an effective way to dissolve your twisted thinking, whether it's emotional reasoning, mind reading, personalization, or other distortions. Remind yourself that you need some cold, hard evidence for a thought to be worthy of your attention. Remember your intuition, hunches, assumptions, conjecture and sixth sense don't count as being credible— none of those would hold up in a real court of law.

So, you gather evidence in support of and against your thought, acting as the prosecutor, defense attorney and judge. You examine the thought from multiple perspectives, in a fair and rational manner. You could put a line in the middle of a piece of paper to weigh the evidence for and against your thought. You ask yourself what the facts are, and what facts you have that the unhelpful thought is totally true and totally not true. Ask yourself if it's possible that this is opinion rather than fact. Ask yourself, "What have other people said about this? Is there another way of seeing it?"

For example, say you find yourself ruminating on the negative thought: "I'll never succeed in my career." To put that thought on trial, ask yourself, "What's the evidence that I'll never succeed?" You must review the past objectively. You may conclude and end up saying, "Well, there's a history of success and a history of failure." That's good objective data. But, and most importantly, how does that add up to *never*? It doesn't. Therefore, the verdict is that the thought has been disproven.

You can also employ the Scientific Method to your thinking. Do research, collect objective data, and analyze it to see if it supports your hypothesis. Reasoning must link the claim and evidence, so you can draw your conclusion. Critical thinking is another way of looking at this, which is an essential skill. It includes rational, skeptical, unbiased analysis, and evaluation of factual evidence.

It's a matter of getting really literal about the kinds of blanket statements we have in our self-talk, not accepting them, and challenging them when they're repeatedly harmful.

## That's possible, but how likely is it?

This works well in calming me since it doesn't deny. It acknowledges that what I'm concerned about is possible. However, the 'how likely' part reminds me that it's a possibility, not a certainty. Usually with the things my brain creates, several unlikely scenarios would need to fall perfectly into place for the worst case to occur, so reminding myself of this is helpful. Looking at impartial statistics is also helpful. For example, airline safety and the percentage of commercial passengers hurt per year, or the percentage of people hit by lightning.

## So what if?

Much of our self-created stress centers around 'what if' scenarios. A great retort to these is simply adding the word 'so' in front of your 'what if'. This gets your mind thinking about how you'll respond instead of just how bad your scenario would be. You'll be surprised with the solutions, contingency plans and ways to improve on the situation you'll come up with. It's usually never as bad as it seems once we start thinking about what we can do make it better. For example, instead of 'what if' I lose my job, you turn that around to, "'So what if' I lose my job? I'll find another. How many jobs have I had in my life? I'm talented and I can do a lot of different things. Many employers will want me."

"So what if" is an effective disarming and non-dramatic phrase to use in some circumstances. You don't want to use it to be stuck in denial. We're again looking for a middle ground of being stuck in the worst-case scenarios and analysis-paralysis and being oblivious to the reality around you. Writer Corrie Ten Boom said, "Worrying does not empty tomorrow of its troubles. It empties today of its strength."

## How much will this matter to me a year from now?

This comes from Richard Carlson, best known as being the author of *Don't Sweat the Small Stuff… and it's all Small Stuff*. He was an inspiration for me and my mentor. I was a certified presenter for his book for a national seminar company years ago. Carlson preached that the vast majority of the daily dramas that were on your mind one year ago today don't matter much now. It's true and a great thing to remind yourself of so you don't get emotionally hooked into the common frustrations we all face.

## I don't know the whole story

We need to remind ourselves that most of the time we just have a hypothesis. We don't have the entire set of facts from other people's perspectives. Most of the time we haven't asked the necessary questions or done the necessary research. For example, you may sense that your boss is ignoring you. He or she may have other things going on, or they trust you, or think if you really need something, you'll ask. Our minds are predetermined to create convincing worst-case scenarios. Simply saying to yourself, "Wait a minute, I don't know the whole story here" can effectively diffuse things.

## What would someone else say about this situation?
## Or, what advice would I give someone else?

Taking the situation out of your own perspective and thinking of how other people would see it is an effective technique. Friends can often make us feel better by rationally giving us other perspectives to challenge our absurd thoughts. We can talk our friends off the crazy ledge frequently but it's hard to give ourselves that same perspective. So, ask yourself, what would some other voices say? What would my best friend think? If my best friend had this thought and I wanted to help him or her see it differently, what would I say? If I had a Hollywood agent, what would he or she tell me? Or a kindly aunt or grandmother? Friends are great at helping us overcome the cognitive distortion of discounting the positive. They can point out factual examples from our present and past where we have demonstrated strength and accomplished things. Think of anyone who believes (or believed) in you and wishes unconditionally for your happiness. Try to mirror what they would say to you.

## Just because I feel it doesn't mean it's true

This is especially pertinent to the emotional reasoning cognitive distortion since that toxic thinking habit mistakes feelings for reality. If you feel anxious, something bad is about to happen. If you feel guilty, it must be your fault. If you feel hopeless, there must be no solution or way out.

How you feel is true for you. I'm not suggesting denying your feelings, but please understand they're not always accurate or based on reality. "My boss wants to see me, so she must be mad" is not an accurate statement just because you feel anxious about it. "Everyone will see I'm sweating and think I'm a freak" is not an accurate statement just because you feel nervous about a presentation. "Because I feel jealous, it proves you're cheating on me" is not an accurate statement. So, ask: What's the evidence that he/she is cheating, besides your own jealousy? What's the evidence he/she hates you? Most of the time, there is none. They're just thoughts.

## It's to be expected

It's helpful to remind ourselves that many of the frustrations we face are completely normal, predictable and to be expected. This allows us to not be so thrown off by them and gives us wisdom and restraint. Some common examples would be, "It's expected that not everyone is going like us," or, "There will be conflict." If you're a teacher, it's to be expected that a percentage of parents are going to be difficult or not fully functional. In the workplace, there will be some poor decisions made by upper management that are out of your control that negatively impact you. If you're a building inspector, it's expected there will be some conflict as some people will not want to do what you're requiring. Not all of us can be flower deliverers who only brighten peoples' day.

Sometimes we need to remind ourselves that this is the profession we've chosen. We have to take the good with the bad. If you're self-employed, it's to be expected that a part of your day will have to be allocated towards marketing. If you're in a marriage, it's expected there will be times when you feel like you can't stand your spouse. If you have kids, it's expected that there will be times when they test you and drive you nuts. The possibilities are endless with this, and you can think of many on your own. The bottom line is, pain in life is inevitable or expected, but misery is optional.

## Reframe it

Give the situation a positive spin. Emulate how a politician or attorney will try to turn things around to show themselves or their client in the best light. Some are great at changing the narrative, being their own spin master, or trying to get the news media to frame the story the way they want it. Do the same thing. Try to find the silver lining, the lesson the challenge taught you, or the good that came out of it. Most of the time we can find this if we look hard enough and ask ourselves the right questions.

I loved the reframing example from the movie *Apollo 13*. Flight Director Gene Kranz played by Ed Harris, overhears two NASA directors discussing the low survival chances for the crippled spacecraft. "This could be the worst disaster NASA has ever experienced," one of them says. "With all due respect, Sir," Kranz intervenes, "I believe this is going to be our finest hour."

Another example of positive reframing was in the movie *Wild,* the story of Cheryl Strayed. Laura Dern's character, playing the mother, is in her kitchen happily humming a song. The character of her daughter is annoyed with her and accuses her of being oblivious to their real situation. She asks her, "What's wrong with you? Why are you happy? Don't you understand that we have nothing, this house is falling apart, we're poor, and that you married an abusive alcoholic A-hole?" I loved her response. She said, "Well, we're rich in love. And do I regret marrying an abusive alcoholic A-hole? No, not for one second. Because I got you. And your brother. See how it works? It isn't easy but it's worth it. Find your best self and hold onto it."

One way you can reframe the end of a relationship or divorce is to tell yourself that you're both wonderful people, and even wonderful parents, but you're just not a wonderful couple.

Children who have Attention Deficit Disorder (ADD) can be hard on themselves and it's easy for their self-esteem to be negatively impacted. It all goes back to how they see themselves. If they see it as there is something wrong with them or they are deficient in some way, it's going to be tougher. To help them reframe their challenges and how they see themselves is to compare their brains to a powerful race car engine with bicycle brakes. They only need to work on strengthening their brakes, so they don't spin out and crash.

For our thoughts that need a mindset shift, the best move is always a positive reframe. Many times, we need to change the story we're telling ourselves about what's happening around us. People can get so attached to their story that they forget they can change it and stop reinforcing and repeating a negative story. Carl Greer has an entire book on this entitled *Change Your Story, Change Your Life*.

This is especially pertinent for people who work in sales. Some struggle with consistently having to put themselves out there, knowing they will face rejection. Cold-calling and dealing with rude clients can be tough. You must have your Mind Right. One thing that works well is reframing every action and cold call as a step towards making more money, putting that money into something that's meaningful for you long-term and brings up positive emotions.

Reframing is often bringing gratitude into the situation. You try to find a "yeah, but" retort. Instead of being frustrated by your commute, "Yeah, but, I'm so glad I have a job to go to and this commute gives me time to get my mind in the right place before I arrive." Or, instead of feeling sorry for yourself for a physical heath challenge, you may reply with, "Yeah, but I'm so glad I still have all my mental faculties." It also acknowledges some truth in what you originally thought, but that there is another side. "Yeah, I did face some rejection today, but it wasn't everyone and I can readjust my approach for tomorrow." You want to go for balance, or at least softening and qualifying the thoughts.

Writing things down takes some time and effort. For the meaningful and repetitive things, it makes sense. Go ahead and make the effort to think it through logically and rationally so you can see how it's so ridiculous. This works well with thoughts you're putting on trial, etc.

With practice you'll do less writing. Your goal is to be able to recognize quicker, and if not ignore the noise, to reframe it sooner so it doesn't grow into a huge thing. After you've done it a few times it gets easier to reframe a disruptive chain of thoughts in your mind without having to have to write it out.

Quick and on-the-spot reframes work well. It's possible to change our emotional patterns just by decisively curtailing our negative thinking and fueling positive thinking.

In addition to what's already been cited in this chapter, here are some responses you can use to interrupt and resist your patterns before your harmful thinking gets too much momentum. It works best to take a deep breath in with your nose and, as you exhale through your mouth, say the response:

- I'll cross that bridge when I come to it.

- One day at a time.

- That's in the past.

- That was then, but this is now.

- The past doesn't dictate the future.

- That's my mother's or father's old negative voice, not mine. (This can help you to keep separation between you and your thoughts.)

- That's ridiculous.

- I can handle it.

- I'm just mind reading (or substitute another cognitive distortion from previous chapter).

- This is my old habit of _____.

- Maybe it will turn out better than I can imagine.

- Is this thought balanced? Is it fair?

- What has helped me in the past when I thought or felt this way?

- What's the worst-case scenario? Can I live with that, or is there anything I can do to improve on it?

- If I were to pretend to do a U-turn on my beliefs or way of seeing this, what might I think or say?

- If one of my kids was thinking this way, what advice would I give to him/her?

- What possible good could come out of thinking this way?

- No, I'm not going down that road. That's a slippery slope.

- I don't need to figure out my entire life in one day.

- Nope, not going there.

- Cancel!

- No, I'm not going to think that way.

- No, I don't want to attract that into my life.

- I've been over this enough. Enough already!

- Is this line of thinking helpful or harmful? Forget about good or bad, or true or false; is it helpful?

- I need to remember the law of diminishing returns since I'm not getting any value or good from this line of thinking, just pain and suffering.

- Cancel! I don't think that way. That's not who I am or who I want to be.

- I'm just starting to have a thought attack. I need to find something else to distract my brain.

- No, I'm not digging myself this hole! Once I start it will be harder to get out of it. I'm putting the shovel down.

- No, I'm not giving him or her this space in my head.

- No, I will not allow him or her to penetrate my mental defenses. They're not worth it.

- It will seem better in the morning. Things always do.

- I don't need to figure anything out right now.

- It's just a thought. It's not a real thing in my life; it's just a thought.

- I don't have to own this thought.

- My brain just creates these crazy thoughts since it's doing its obsolete job.

- Just because this thought popped into my head doesn't mean I have to dwell on it.

- I'm not a licensed fortune teller so I have to stop predicting the future.

- I'm not going to write the story of my future before I've lived it (unless I'm writing it in an awesomely positive manner).

- I must incorporate my equal-time rule— a minimum of equal time between thinking about what I do want and what I don't want.

- Is this how I want things to go, or don't want things to go?

- Don't think that, think this…

- I'm not going there since I don't want that to come true and

I don't want to create a negative self-fulfilling prophecy.

- That's a stupid thought. I'm not saying that I'm stupid, just that the thought my brain created is stupid.

- Is this thought from the unhealthy, dysfunctional part of me or the healthy, functional and rational part?

- Is the thought "I should do this" my own expectation, or my organization's? Has anyone explicitly said to me that I'm expected to do this at this time of day?

- Unless I ask, I have no idea what they think about me. I'm not a mind reader.

- If I'm going to be making an assumption anyway, I'm going to make the assumption that's best for my health and peace of mind.

- It's perfectly normal to feel this way with what I'm currently faced with. Most people in my situation would feel the same way. There's no need to blame or judge myself.

- "It's all good." I use this one when my noise is starting up at night or the morning, as my brain starts to scan for danger and attempts to come up with reasons why my life is a disaster. I just keep repeating 'It's all good' to remind myself that everything is fine, to keep it at bay, and not get into it.

- Everything always works out.

You can probably think of many others and identify a few favorites that work for you. You can use these as anchor thoughts or sayings to keep returning back to when your noise is getting harmful.

# 9. Why Quiet the Noise

Most people agree with the statement that they "think too much," and can relate more to mental exhaustion than physical exhaustion. The 50,000 thoughts a day that we think (on-average), all vying for attention and trying to convince us that they're important and worthy of our careful analysis, can be exhausting. Some people believe the more intelligent they are, the more thoughts they have, and might average more than 50,000 a day.

Some people are too smart for their own good and overthink, overanalyze and over-explain just about everything. We can allow our brains to be on all the time: running, spinning, obsessing, and getting caught up in analysis paralysis. This is what Buddhists call the "monkey mind," the mind that races, is bored and anxious, and skips unhappily from feeling to feeling, trying to outrun those that are least pleasant. This can be a vicious cycle since the more you have a "busy mind," the more stimulation you seek, and the more stimulation you get, the busier your mind becomes.

Technology does not help and has been shown to stimulate the brain, release chemicals, and activate the amygdala. Facebook and Instagram are particularly challenging since the apps fool our brain into believing that loved ones surround us. Users secrete oxytocin, the "love hormone," when viewing touching stories or trying moments. Since our brains evolved thousands of years before photography, it fails on many levels to recognize the difference between photographs and real people. Dopamine is released when viewing attractive images or when caught up in the excitement of our posts being liked. If negative messages are received on social media or if we get caught up in comparing ourselves, we can feel bad and then cortisol, the stress hormone, may to be released. The amount of anxiety, depression and FOMO (fear of missing out) that Instagram causes teenagers is outrageous.

According to Apple, we are compelled to check our phone every 11 minutes and 15 seconds, on average.[19] Do you ever check the Screen Time app on your phone to see how much time you're spending on it or how many times you unlock it per day? The dangers of technology addiction are real, and it's not an accident but purposely engineered by the designers of our devices and social media sites. According to a recent study, staying off Facebook for even one week has been shown to significantly increase happiness.[20] Teens who spent more than a few hours a day online were found to be twice as likely to be unhappy, depressed and anxious than those who spent less than an hour a day. Cold turkey may not be realistic, but moderation is key.

With all this mental stimulation and information surrounding us, we need to disconnect, detach, and shut everything down periodically. Wouldn't it be great if there was a switch on the back of our heads and we could just turn it off?

It's also important to recognize that many people have informal activities or routines that quiet their mind and helps them to relax. Whenever you totally immerse yourself in an activity and focus on what you're doing in the present moment, you are both quieting and getting a break from the noise by relegating it to the background. Afterwards, you may be surprised at how much time has gone by. If someone tells me, for example, that gardening relaxes him/her, I like to ask, "What do you think about while you're gardening?" The answer is, inevitably, "Nothing at all. I'm just focused on the gardening." BINGO! That's exactly the goal. Another way to describe it is they're doing the gardening mindfully.

There are so many examples to include: exercising, doing a thousand-piece puzzle, art or music, Sudoku, Zentangle, yoga, binging on shows or movies, computer games, cooking or cleaning, etc. Yoga has the added physical benefits of flexibility, raising your heart rate, and sweat. It's almost a prerequisite to be mindful and in the moment while doing yoga since you need your entire focus to maintain many of the challenging poses and stretches.

There are constructive and destructive ways to accomplish this quieting of the noise. For example, one of the most-cited reasons why people go to casinos or gamble is to "get a break and escape from life". I like to ask, "A break from what? Their life or their thoughts (the noise) about their life, hence their anxiety about their life?" Some of us need to brainstorm on more positive ways to quiet things down.

Since this book is on navigating mental noise, I'm taking a

deeper dive into the mental technique of meditation. With meditation, you block off a period of time to do nothing but sit up straight with your eyes closed (with most forms) and with the specific intent to quiet or ignore your noise. Meditation is the closest thing to a mental turn-off switch that we'll find.

I wish someone had taught me about meditation when I was much, much younger. I remember when I was single, going to a Caribbean Club Med vacation in the Turks and Caicos. My goal was to relax, of course. I wasn't very mindful back then and just took my stressful thoughts from Boston to the Caribbean with me. Without good strategies to quiet or ignore the noise, I would have been better off going to a meditation retreat. Or, I should have brought John Cabot-Zinn's book, *Wherever You Go, There You Are,* with me and read that on the beach.

Doesn't it seem like so many people are afraid of, and try to avoid, boredom? But breaking through that resistance and leaning into boredom and resting the mind is a game changer. The dichotomy is: The more you feel as though you can't do it, then the more you need to do it. All of our electronic stimulation and gaming seems to create more anxiety since our brains don't get used to having wind down and quiet time. Hence our brains will look to avoid this state at all costs and will create more and more anxiety to stay out of this state. Nowadays, if I'm feeling uncomfortable and my mind is racing, I know one of the foremost reasons why is that I haven't done anything for a few days to quiet my mind.

Taking a respite, not engaging or following any of your thoughts, and letting your mind go into neutral is crucial. Every so often we just need to give it a rest. Doing it consistently keeps putting the noise in its place. It reminds you that you are the master and your brain and thoughts are the servant. Meditation keeps the noise to the back pages, or as I like to say, the legal notices section.

Meditation reminds you to be here now, in the present moment. You become accustomed to living in the moment, which is vital since so much of our noise is related to thoughts about the past or future. Eckhart Tolle, in his great book *The Power of Now,* tells us, "Realize deeply that the present moment is all you ever have. Make the *now* the primary focus of your life."

Meditation played a key role in the memorable saga of 12 young soccer players and their coach who were trapped in a flooded cave in Thailand a while back. Once they were located, a complicated international rescue operation was underway. This rescue through a challenging exit route fascinated people around the world. What people forget is that they were lucky to be found; and what they were doing when they were found.

After rainwater flooded the cave they went hiking in, blocking their exit, they were located by a diving team 10 days later on a muddy incline. This was about one-kilometer underground and two kilometers from the cave's entrance.

Can you imagine, all those days without food, fresh water, or contact from the outside world? Waiting in a dark cave for a rescue that may not happen. They had no stimulation or distractions, only their thoughts.

Their coach, Ekapol Chantawong, was a former novice Buddhist monk who still meditates daily. He taught the boys meditation so they could stay calm, emotionally balanced, and preserve their energy through this ordeal. In the process, he gave them the vital tools they needed in order to learn how to tap into their own tranquility and inner stillness. He taught them how to keep *themselves* calm, a huge distinction. When the divers discovered them, they were amazed to find them meditating. They were just calmly sitting there waiting. No one was crying or emotional. Many of the parents credited the coach and his approach towards the crisis as being the crucial factor in keeping the team alive so they could be rescued.

Meditation is one of the best things you can do for your health. It has been medically proven to have a tremendous positive effect on your physical and mental well-being, as well as the structure and function of your brain. This is now indisputable, thanks to scientific evidence. A breakthrough 2011 study, led by a team at the Massachusetts General Hospital and Harvard University neuroscientist Dr. Sara Lazar, conducted brain scans of meditation participants before and after an eight-week mindful meditation program. What they found was amazing— actual structural changes in the brain— with an increased concentration of gray matter in brain regions associated with learning, memory, perspective, and regulation of emotions. Also, the amygdala shrunk, which makes us less reactive and sensitive towards perceived threats and problems, and less negative overall.[21]

It's becoming more common for meditation to be combined with psychotherapy, especially cognitive behavioral therapy (CBT), which makes sense since both meditation and CBT share the objective of giving people more clear perspectives on irrational and self-defeating thoughts. A newer generation of CBT is ACT, which is Acceptance and Commitment Therapy. ACT teaches you to just notice, accept, and embrace your private events, especially previous unwanted ones. The core concept is that psychological suffering is caused by experiential avoidance. If you're afraid of or nervous about things, you will not do it. This deprives you the opportunity for learning and growth.

An eye-opening study from researchers at Lund University in Sweden showed group mindful meditation to be just as effective as CBT for treating individuals suffering from anxiety, depression and severe stress responses.[22] Meditation is more affordable and convenient. Evidence of the efficacy of mindfulness-based treatments continues to grow, and there are now nearly 500 scientific studies on mindfulness meditation and the brain in the National Institute of Health's PubMed database.

Meditating can help to get your brain more like Albert Einstein's. His brain was removed and studied shortly after his death in 1955. According to Florida State University researchers, Einstein's

Prefrontal Cortex was incredibly well-developed— exhibiting "densely packed gray matter"— while covering "much more surface area" than the typical average brain.[23] A 2005 study by neuroscientists also discovered that the brains of veteran meditation practitioners also had much more thickness, density, and activity within their prefrontal cortex— just like Einstein's. [24]

The Prefrontal Cortex is key to our success and well- being. It's really the CEO, or happiness center, and overall thought orchestrator of the brain. It's been shown to be underactive in people with many mental health issues, including bipolar disorder and depression. This is devastating since the prefrontal cortex is a kind of surge protector, which helps to modulate the responses of the amygdala. In veteran meditators, the cortex has weaker connections to the amygdala, making it less likely for any hard-wired reactivity to overwhelm the logical part of the brain. Conversely, meditation strengthens the attention centers of the cortex, which creates a distance from anxiety. This allows us to experience anxiety with less judgment and drama.

Meditating also has cognitive benefits; you think better. This is why meditation and mindfulness training are becoming much more popular and valued in corporate environments and I'm asked to do it frequently. It can't be considered a "nice to have" for executives; it's a must have. Think of the phrase, the "corporate athlete". Most of us are not evaluated in the workplace based on our physical strength. Most of us are immersed in knowledge work— processing information and making decisions. We're using our brain.

David Allen, the creator of the time management method knowns as "Getting Things Done", says, "Your ability to generate power is inversely proportional to your ability to relax." Since our brains are the most important determiner of our workplace success, what are we doing to train it, or to improve it? For far too many people, the answer is nothing, or not enough. Specifically, meditating boosts the executive functions of the frontal lobes to include your ability to manage time, pay attention, switch focus, plan, organize, concentrate,

remember details, and control impulses. Don't we all need more of those abilities in today's workplace?

Meditation also boosts serotonin, the "mood stabilizing" neurotransmitter to higher levels. It has been proven by countless studies to be even superior to running for naturally boosting endorphins and dopamine. Meditation is the best tool to get your feel-good brain chemicals going in the healthiest way possible. It also helps you to become more resilient and modulate the normal challenges of life. I've never heard of an addict who meditates.

Meditation also helps facilitate creativity. Most of the thoughts we're having today we had yesterday and will have tomorrow. This doesn't leave enough space in our mind for new thoughts or new solutions to our problems to arise. When we back off from working on a problem, we change what we're doing and our context. This activates different areas of our brain where solutions may be found.

Research has shown that daydreaming, or doing something monotonous and not requiring much thought, flips you to autopilot and you're more likely to have a creative epiphany and an "a-ha!" moment. Your unconscious can work on something else and your mind goes wandering, leaving your brain to quietly play an unconstrained game of free association. This kind of daydreaming relaxes the prefrontal cortex and switches on the rest of your brain's "default mode network" (DMN), clearing the pathways that connect different regions of your brain. With your cortex loosened up and your DMN switched on, you can make new, creative connections that your conscious mind would have dismissed.[25]

In creativity research, they refer to it as the three Bs— the bathtub, the bed and the bus— places where ideas have famously and suddenly emerged. Many highly successful people swear by this and will schedule time to drive aimlessly for an hour or more to do their best thinking and get their best ideas. Very few people would say they get their best ideas in front of a computer screen.

Sadly, people seldom let their minds rest; they're usually on their devices. I have to keep reminding my kids to get off them in the car, and that it's good for you to be bored. Our inability to stare out a window and daydream is detrimental on many levels. Addiction to stimulation and devices is rampant. What about the bathtub? There have been too many instances lately of people dying from dropping their phones into tub and electrocuting themselves. What about the bathroom? A survey conducted by the marketing company 11Mark, called "IT in the Toilet," found that about 75 percent of Americans admitted to using their mobile phones while in the bathroom.

All of this makes the famous quote by Blaise Pascal, "All of humanity's problems stem from man's inability to sit quietly in a room alone," even more applicable. It's unbelievable that this was written in the 1660's! What would Pascal say today?

People are clamoring to find a room to be able to sit quietly alone. In South Korea— one of the most overworked societies with a hyper-competitive work and school culture— a growing trend is to check yourself into 'prison' to relax. These are jail-themed retreats, where you can escape the outside world of technology— calls, and people making demands on you— in solitary confinement.

I've completed a weekend meditation retreat where talking isn't allowed, even during mealtimes. These highly structured boot camp type of interventions to get a respite from our overly-stimulated and busy lives are only going to get more popular. Maybe I could buy a closed prison and convert it to a retreat center. Since we Americans have the highest prison population rate in world, that might be difficult. Alcatraz?

With the growing body of research, you should be convinced of the logical mental, physical and psychological performance benefits of meditation, and to commit to trying it and sticking with it, even if you find it difficult. In the next chapter, we'll learn how to do it.

.

# 10. How to Quiet the Noise

There are many distinctive styles, forms, or types of meditation, but they all have one thing in common— a focal point for your attention. You need a focal point to place your attention, as opposed to paying attention to your constant dialogue of noise, thoughts and mental chatter. Focal points can be separated into two main categories. The first is more of a passive, quiet focal point. The second is more of an active one, as in chanting, repeating a mantra or listening to guidance.

Meditation can also generally have one or two objectives. The first is to gain the physiological benefits from a cessation, or marked reduction, of mental activity. Electrical brain waves can be measured with an EEG, or an electroencephalogram; there will be less Beta brain waves and more Alpha and Theta waves during meditation.

The second objective is to train the brain to focus only on what you want it to, so you can develop enhanced focus, concentration, and mental toughness. Both objectives help you to be aware of your constant wandering, or monkey mind. By removing all other stimulation and sitting with your dialogue, it's much easier to notice it.

For the first objective of meditation, here are eight simple steps:

1/ Start off slowly. A goal to meditate four times a week for 15 minutes is reasonable. From even this small amount of time you will notice many positive benefits. The interesting dichotomy is that the more you think you can't do this, or can't find the time to do this, or the more it drives you crazy, the more you need to do it.

2/ Don't expect it to be perfect; be realistic with yourself. The main reason why people give up on meditation is they get frustrated and think they're not doing it right. The intention is the most crucial element. Don't place unrealistic expectations on yourself. Don't think you're going to suddenly levitate off the ground or see some sort of tunnel or white light! It's called a practice because we have to keep practicing.

3/ Find a quiet place with no interruptions. Easier said than done for a lot of us. You may need to be creative.

4/ Give yourself permission to take the time to do this. It's helpful to say to yourself, "Just for the next 15 minutes (or whatever your timeframe is), I don't need to figure anything out. I am enough just the way I am right now. I don't need to improve anything or work on anything. This is my break from all that— a break from my mind and it's constant stream of thoughts."

I use a timer so I don't have to worry about the time. There are many apps nowadays that also have timers, and I've listed some at the end of this chapter.

5/ Choose a focal point for where you will place your attention. Be creative and find the focal point that works best for you. It could be a visualization of a peaceful place, continually repeating a mantra (a phrase or saying), focusing on the process of your breathing, or listening to something that guides you with some of the apps listed below. For those with a spiritual connection, the focal point could be a prayer. Some say that praying is talking with God, and meditating is quieting down to listen for the answers.

There are many options here, and I will explain some others in greater depth, but my personal preference is to pay attention to the process of my breathing. This is what is commonly associated with the phrase "mindful meditation". Sit up straight, start to take some slow, deep breaths, and simply pay attention to the process of breathing. Pay attention to where you feel the breath on each inhalation, when your chest expands, and your lungs fill up with air. Also pay attention to where you feel the breath when you exhale and your lungs collapse. It is preferable to exhale longer than you inhale since that activates the parasympathetic, or rest and digest nervous system. Don't get hung-up on that detail. Just pay close attention to every nuance of this breathing process.

6/ When thoughts arise, simply notice the thought and gently return back to your focal point. Thoughts are absolutely going to arise. The normal and natural state of your mind is always thinking, or wondering. We've all heard the phrase, "Let it go." But a more accurate phrase for this practice is, "Let it be." Just let it be. Let the thoughts be. A wise meditation teacher once told me, "When it comes, don't run away from it. When it leaves, don't chase after it." A thought is a thought is a thought. Nothing more, nothing less. Thoughts can be very seductive; it's easy to allow them to draw you in and take you down a road where you don't want to go.

What's most important with meditation is not the initial thought that enters your mind, but what you do next. Do you have the self-discipline to let the thought be and gently return to your focal point? No thought can grow unless you give it your attention and energy. You don't resist, you don't cancel, you don't go through the mental snowball melt, you don't put effort into replacing the thoughts. That would only result in getting yourself riled up, and creating more thoughts, which defeats the purpose. No thought can grow unless you validate it. Simply resolve to not pay any attention to them and let them be in the background. You just notice and return. Notice and return.

Returning to the train analogy, think of a train station with a multitude of tracks emanating from it in different directions. The goal is to not let any trains of thought leave the station. It's much harder to stop a train that's moving and has built up momentum. Don't let the train build up momentum and start to move down the track. If it does, get off at the next stop and return to the train station.

7/ Be gentle with yourself when noticing and returning. The key is to notice and return gently, in an effortless way. You're simply tolerating or observing the endless spontaneous wondering of your brain without getting too involved, just letting thoughts pass by in an effortless way. Imagine you are standing near the edge of a fast-moving stream with all sorts of leaves, twigs or other objects in it. As it all flows by, you don't want to place your focus on just one object; you want to have a softer focus with your eyes and notice them all flow by the entire stream, and to just recognize it for what it is— an endless stream. Another analogy is to imagine the spontaneous wandering of your brain being on a large movie screen, but you are sitting back several rows in the theater and just being a detached observer as the film plays on.

Being gentle also means not berating yourself for having certain thoughts. It means not saying anything to yourself similar to, "Ugh! Why am I thinking this way?" Or, "I'm never going to able to do this!" None of that is helpful. Sometimes I say to myself, "There's a thought; okay, time to come back to the breathing." You may want to create a gentle reminder phrase that you feel comfortable with. However you do it, just quickly return back to the focal point before your thoughts have a chance to reign you in and gain momentum.

8/ Grasp that you never stop your mind; you just notice the thoughts and return. Just like our hearts naturally beat, our minds naturally think. Long-time practitioners still have a dialogue of thoughts happening. If all you do for a 15-minute period is just notice and return, that's great. At least you are not letting anything snowball. The key is in the returning. Eventually it gets easier to marginalize your thinking more in the background instead of the foreground, and it gets easier to pay less attention and not attach yourself to the dialogue.

That's it. Those are the eight steps. It doesn't need to be any more complicated; you don't need anything else. Many meditation gurus have unnecessarily complicated the process of meditation by using incomprehensible jargon about its practice and goals.

If all you did for 15 minutes was return back to your focal point 100 times, that's fine. Put a positive spin on it. Tell yourself that you had 100 repetitions of practice returning and you're building up that muscle. If you were building up your bicep muscle, you'd feel great about 100 repetitions. You're getting better at it each time. Remember, there's a reason this is called a practice.

For those of us who struggle with this and have a hard time quieting down the noise, an alternative is to have a very active focal point that takes even more of your attention. This method does result in more mental activity since the focal point is so complex that it creates thoughts. However, you're making more of an effort to engage with and redirect thoughts onto something else— where you want it to go.

This also helps to train your brain and increase its ability to focus and concentrate, which can be the second objective of meditation. I employ it when I'd like to fall asleep and there is something pressing on my mind that I need to stop thinking about.

A common approach to this is that, in addition to paying

attention to breathing, you also count the breath by saying to yourself what number you're on. It's been proven that it's more relaxing to count down as opposed to counting up. That's why if you've ever had anesthesia, they always say count down from 10 to one, never count up from one to 10.

Begin on an inhalation, and while taking your first breath, say, "Inhale 100." While you exhale that first breath, say, "Exhale 99." And then, "Inhale 98, exhale 97, inhale 96, exhale 95," etc. You can also visualize the words and numbers. You can even visualize the inhales in one color and the exhales in another.

An even more elaborate and effective focal point is to add an element of math to the counting and count down by three. Start at 250 since it's a higher number and not divisible by three. You begin at, "Inhale 250, exhale 247, inhale 244, exhale 241," etc. While I'm counting, I really need to pay attention. Sometimes I lose count of the number and I simply restart at "Inhale 250." Is this particularly relaxing? No, not really. But does it give my brain something else to do instead of dwelling on something? Does it help me fall asleep? Absolutely. If the dialogue in my mind consists of asking myself, "What number am I on?" it's preferable to, "What's wrong with my life?" particularly at midnight. I randomly vary this and may start at "Inhale 251" since it's easy to get too used to the math.

Occasionally, in the middle of the exercise I will vary it by starting at a random high number, say 783, and start counting down by seven. Until I have the math done I keep saying to myself, "Inhale

783, inhale 783," even though I'm both inhaling and exhaling. Once I have the answer, then I say, "Exhale 776." Another option is to make sure my exhales are twice as long as my inhales.

Visualizing a relaxing or enjoyable experience you've had can also be an effective focal point. Make it as vivid as possible with as much detail as possible. One Vietnam War POW said what helped him cope with his isolation and trauma was imagining playing golf at his favorite course every day. He visualized all the details of each tee, fairway, and green and went through each stroke and step. This was powerful for him. Today we have virtual reality technology which does most of this work for us. This lessens our ability to practice envisioning things.

Another focal point variation can be a phrase that you repeat. There are many options here. Since we're trying to be in the present moment, what are you doing in the moment if you're sitting with your eyes closed? You're definitely breathing; at least you'd better be. You can make that part of your phrase. With each inhalation you can say to yourself, "This breath." With each exhale you say to yourself, "Now." You can also experiment with visualizing those words as you're silently saying them.

Another phrase could be playing around with the word 'nothing.' I sometimes like to think of it as, while I'm doing this practice, I am doing nothing and thinking about nothing. No things. No things to think about or do. I relate the word 'things' with thoughts. So, I will repeat the phrase 'no thing' or 'no things' while

I'm inhaling and exhaling. Sometimes we need to say, "The heck with mindfulness, I need some mindlessness." Just nothing in my mind.

One of my favorite scenes from the 1999 movie *Office Space* was when the main character, after being stuck in a calm trance from an occupational hypnotherapist, was asked what he did all day. His response was, "Absolutely nothing, and it was everything I thought it could be." Many people get annoyed when you're trying to engage with someone who's being quiet and the response you get back when you ask them what they're thinking is, "Nothing." If that's true, then it's great. Thinking about nothing can be a great thing.

Some of the mantras and chanting that are used with various forms of meditation can become quite elaborate and require a lot of our attention and breathing. This does work well for some people.

Another form of meditation is walking meditation. This is usually with a group of people indoors in a safe area and you're walking in a line in a slow and deliberate manner. Your eyes are almost closed, looking down at the feet of the person in front of you. You don't want a lot of visual stimulation and to be looking all around the room. You feel all the sensations of walking— the weight shift as your heel hits the floor and has you roll onto the front of your foot. I also add a phrase as I'm doing this. As my left foot hits the ground I say, "This step," and as my right foot hits I say, "Now." There are lots of outdoor nature settings that can easily calm the mind. There is a mile and ¼ long breakwater with large granite boulders in Cape Cod that I walk on every summer with my kids. They're mostly flat but have plenty of gaps in between them. If you're not paying attention and planning where each step is going to land, you're risking major injury. It's great exercise in getting out of the head and into the feet, and the sensation of them landing on the rocks.

You'll probably try a few focal points and periodically switch them around.

The mind is like an untrained puppy. You have to be very firm but very gentle with it. If you were training a puppy to go to the bathroom on a newspaper on the floor, and the puppy went elsewhere, you'd simply pick the puppy up and put him back on the newspapers. If he does it again, you'd pick him up, put him back on the newspaper. You wouldn't explain to the puppy why he should go to the newspaper and get into a protracted debate over motives and intentions. Just like with meditation, you just notice and return. No long explanations, no attention, no energy given to it.

Another way to learn meditation is to find a good teacher, which is mostly in a group setting.

A new technological tool to help learn meditation is an EEG headband, which is now finally available for purchase. This is a small band that sits easily on your forehead, above your ears, that measures brain activity through sensors. The version that I use is a product called Muse, which works very well. You receive biofeedback data since it connects to your devices through Bluetooth and it allows you fascinating insight to what's going on in your brain. In one of the Muse exercises, you hear the sound of ocean waves. When your brain has wandered from focusing on your breathing and is becoming more active, the nature sound of the waves becomes louder, and then softer as your mind gets calmer.

This type of real-time feedback is priceless. It's the equivalent of having a meditation assistant, or brain-wave coach, gently tap you on the shoulder when you start to wander. When your brain activity is calm for a set amount of time, you hear the sound of a bird as a reinforcement. After the session, I can scroll through a timed bar graph to see my exact brain waves— when my brain was active, neutral, or calm along with my recovery points, which is when I caught myself and calmed by brain waves by returning my focus back to my breathing. Muse also quantifies how well you did by assigning points based on the percentage of time your brain was either active, neutral or calm. See the screenshot image on the next page.

Wearing the headband has made my meditations more effective. It made me realize that some of the time when I thought I was meditating, I wasn't. The example above— my attempt to meditate at 9:44 a.m. — wasn't very successful. My brain was mostly neutral or active and the statistics show that. I was either daydreaming or contemplating something. It may have been pleasant, but it wasn't meditation. It makes it easier to learn what the experience of doing it right— being calm, centered, and having a still brain— *feels like* since you get this objective data. I like to make a game of it and challenge myself to see how low I can go with my brain waves and how long I can stay there.

I also want to see if I can extend the gap between my thoughts— that time when there is just nothing.

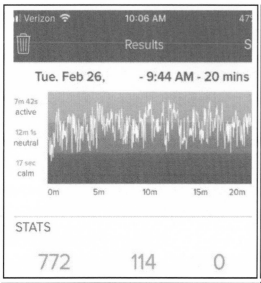

My next attempt at a 20-minute meditation session, right after the first one at 10:06 a.m., felt more successful and the data on the second set of images backed that up- compare the two.

If you take all the spiritual connotations and jargon out of meditation, isn't it supposed to be about a cessation, or marked reduction, of mental activity? If I wear this headband that measures my electrical brain waves, there is no second-guessing or confusion on how I'm doing, or if I'm doing it right. Meditation is an exercise. We wear devices to give us benchmarks for physical activity such as our pulse or number of steps; why not in order to objectively see how we're doing during mental exercise?

This type of technology is only going to get more popular and accessible. But it's not for everyone. For some, thinking about how you're meditating, or being anxious about the volume of the nature sounds, just creates more thoughts and defeats the purpose. Sometimes we need a break from measuring and evaluating everything, especially if you struggle with perfectionism. There are so many devices and apps available to us to measure so many body functions. Apple is looking to make an impact on health measurements with its watches, which includes an EKG measurement to detect heart irregularities. This can become too much and obsessive. There have been some recent studies linking the data overload of activity trackers with increased anxiety and obsessive thoughts, decreased enjoyment of whatever pastime someone is trying to quantify, and an increase in self-criticism.

I don't wear the band every time I meditate or keep the volume on if I do wear it. Once you learn what it feels like to have a calm or still brain, you may not need it; just like when you learn what it feels like to be in your target heart range, you may not need to wear a heart monitor. At times it's nice to just do the best you can without any concerns or evaluation of results.

An alternative method to calm your brain is a flotation, or sensory deprivation tank. You float effortlessly in the water since it has a lot of Epsom salt in it. It provides some of the deepest meditations I've experienced. It's easier for the brain to rest since it is not getting much input. There's little for your body to feel, see or hear. You can leave the door open if you feel closed in. There are also options for more of a pool-like setting.

With any of these techniques, you're reinforcing to your brain that you're calm and safe, and you're not experiencing an emergency. You're activating the relaxation response, the opposite of the flight and flight response. This is mediated by the autonomic nervous system and involves decreases in respiration, heart rate and stress hormones. You're training your brain to be calmer, to call for less cortisol, and to call for it less frequently. Over time, you become a less-reactive person and have more wisdom and self-restraint.

Resting your mind, putting it in neutral, teaches you to develop a different relationship with your thoughts. It can help train you to recognize that you are not your thoughts and your thoughts are not you. If you do this consistently, there can be more of a barrier between you and the outside world, a barrier of inner peace and serenity. You can be surrounded by craziness, but with a firewall around you, you won't let as much in.

One of the most powerful things to develop in life is a different relationship with your thoughts. Imagine lying in bed, trying to go to sleep, and your brain begins to roil with anxiety-producing thoughts, but you're more detached from the thoughts. You just notice the thoughts and say, "Hey, I don't have to react to these. I don't have to respond to that and go there." It's like becoming a detached observer of your thoughts. It's powerful to be able to just notice the thoughts going on in the background, without these thoughts having the same emotional charge to them. It's a very powerful place to be.

Here are some mindfulness apps and websites that you might find helpful:

| | |
|---|---|
| Headspace | Mindifi |
| Calm | Relax Melodies.com |
| MINDBODY | Take a Break |
| Aura | Worry Watch |
| Breethe | MindShift |
| Simply Being | Pacifica |
| Omvana | mindful.org |
| Buddhify | Everyday-mindfulness.org |
| Mindbliss | Calm.com |
| Stop Breathe & Think | Daily Yoga |

# 11. Rewire Your Brain and Create Your Own Noise

Much was said about negative noise, but the exciting news is our brains are learning organs. We can use our minds to change our brain. It's called neuroplasticity. Neuroplasticity offers us hope for change and improvement. You may have heard the term, but what does neuroplasticity mean?

It's an umbrella term referring to the ability of our brains to reorganize itself, both physically and functionally, throughout our life due to our experiences, environment, thinking, behavior, emotions, or injury. Once thought to be "hardwired" by adulthood, the brain is actually "soft wired" by experience— meaning it's possible to rewire your brain to improve everything from your mood, memory, relationships, sleeping habits, and more.

With the relatively recent ability to visually "see" into the brain allowed by functional magnetic resonance imaging, science has confirmed the remarkable adaptations of the brain.

Neuroplasticity is logical. How else are we able to learn anything new? We're constantly changing and evolving because our brains are constantly changing and evolving.

Look at how our brain attempts to heal when injured or damaged. Although individual neurons may be damaged beyond repair, the brain attempts to repair itself. New connections or new neural pathways compensate for the damage to restore some functionality.

The brain undergoes drastic changes during pregnancy and motherhood. Women almost gain superpowers when they become mothers: heightened sensory perception, enhanced problem-solving skills, superior multitasking abilities, and powerful intuition. It's also normal to feel emotional changes such as feeling anxious and overwhelmed; these biological brain changes are happening and protective instincts are kicking in. Meditation also brings on changes; Chapter 9 illustrates the positive neural plasticity structural changes in the brain from this practice, to including shrinking the size of the amygdala.

Not all neuroplasticity and brain changes are positive. An obvious example is addiction— where the pleasure centers of the brain are essentially hijacked. Eventually, only addictive behavior brings the addict any sense of satisfaction, or at least some relief from pain. This is both a biochemical process since the drugs themselves that the addict takes affect the brain's biochemistry, and also a process of habit. The addict's brain becomes hardened to the addictive act becoming the exclusive source of pleasure— not good experiences, family, friends, or a job well done. Currently, methadone, buprenorphine, and Vivitrol have been proven effective at curbing cravings and lessening withdrawal symptoms. Sadly, some people reject the idea of taking these medications with a common but inaccurate view: "I don't want to trade one addiction for another."

Experienced-based or self-directed neuroplasticity is the part that is under our control, and where the area for improvement is. You strengthen positive brain pathways that work for you, essentially re-wiring. It's exciting that brain changes can be generated by mental activity alone. Something as seemingly insubstantial as thought, with no outside input, can alter neuronal connections and the brains structure. The brain takes the shape of what it rests on. If it rests on negativity, it reinforces that and just becomes more negative.

First a primer on how this all works. We have trillions of brain cells, called neurons, and they communicate with one another via synaptic transmission— one brain cell releases a chemical (neurotransmitter, aka brain communicators) that the next brain cell absorbs. This communication process is known as neuronal firing. A typical neuron makes about 5,000 connections with other neurons, leaving us a total of about 500 trillion synapses.

What's meant by the popular phrase "Neurons that fire together, wire together" is that when specific neurons communicate frequently, the connection between them strengthens. Messages that travel the same pathway in the brain repeatedly begin to transmit faster, like a superhighway. With enough repetition, they become almost automatic.

To understand how the brain strengthens neural connections, look to a string of holiday lights. When it's time to find them for the holiday season in our house, they're usually all mushed together and just about impossible to untangle. Think of your brain as a very compacted mass of trillions of tiny lights, most of which are connected to each other with strings, resulting in thousands (if not millions) of strings of lights correlating with our habits and experiences in all areas of our life.

When we start to think about something, there's a chemical reaction in the brain that's like plugging in one of these strings of lights. As you think about something, positive or negative, you turn on a string of lights related to that topic. The more you think, feel and act the same way, the faster the lights turn on and the brighter they glow. Frequently travelled neuronal pathways are more efficient.

As we engage in the habit or line of thinking over and over again, the pathway becomes well-worn or stronger. This is similar to creating a rut in a dirt road by continually driving over the same spot that's easy to fall back into. The string of lights related to driving a car at 50 years old is much brighter and faster than the string you had at 17 years old. If you also drive the same route every day, that habit becomes ingrained and you know which way to go without having to think about it or even be very aware of it.

Many of us have negative thought patterns that continually replay or loop around in our minds. As we ruminate on them they get stronger and appear more real and relevant. These can become superhighways for depression or other problems. This is how automatic or unconscious negative thoughts can escape our awareness. They've become a familiar habit.

I can remember my old "Sunday night feeling" of anxiety that I picked up in childhood, dreading the upcoming week. That was with me for many years, but was just old programming, a habit of old ruts of negative neural networks. This is why we have to be careful not to reinforce anything that we don't want to be true. We have to be aware of these ruts and address them since stress also activates a gene that attaches to brain DNA that can cause abnormalities and other emotional difficulties.

Stress and cortisol in moderation is not harmful; it is motivating. A great resource for this is Robert Sapolsky's book *Why Zebras Don't Get Ulcers.* The Zebras have short periods of intense stress when being chased by a lion, but then there are longer refractory periods when they relax. They don't have our ability to think about the past or ponder the future, so they don't get the physiological stress that humans do. Too often that human ability is more of a curse than a blessing. Too many of us hardly ever truly relax.

Being in a state of chronic stress rewires the brain, but obviously not in a positive way. Stress changes brain architecture differently, depending on how long it lasts. The problems arise when stress is either too intense at one moment, as in a violent attack, or too sustained, as in long-term poverty, neglect, or abuse.

Each neuron has tree-like branches, called dendrites, which are used to communicate with other neurons. With chronic or intense stress, a harmful process called excitotoxicity can occur in which a superabundance of glutamate makes a neuron fire sooner than it should and triggers a cascade of signals inside the cell, damaging its structure. This also allows excess calcium, which activates enzymes that break down the neuron. This canopy of branches shrinks, like a plant doused with herbicide. First the "twigs," called spines, disappear. After prolonged stress, whole branches recede. In depressed brains, many areas are shrunken and underactive, including part of the prefrontal cortex and the hippocampus. But neurons in the amygdala expand like overgrown shrubbery. Being stressed keeps the brain in survival mode and activates the limbic system, boosting connections there and weakening them in the cortex. Perspective is altered, our ability to recall similar situations and creatively formulate plans to find solutions is diminished. The limbic system can seize control and drown out the rational part of us. You become more emotional and your ability to handle future stress effectively is diminished. It's like a bell. The more time you stay stressed, the more sensitive your stress bell becomes. It will not only ring more easily, but ring louder, which keeps the cycle going, and the brain in a near-constant survival mode.

People are differently vulnerable, depending on genes and on prior life experience. This is because we all perceive the stress differently. But subjected to the trauma of war, a bad breakup, or a bout of homelessness, a person with a genetic predisposition may find his or her mind stuck in a loop of chronic fear or depression. The bottom line is: *chronic stress is to mental illness as cigarettes are to lung cancer.*

Rewiring has been news-worthy lately, and people ask, "How do I rewire?" Well, first of all, it's important to grasp that we're already re-wiring. As we live our lives and have various experiences, some connections are strengthened while others are eliminated in a process known as synaptic pruning. Neurons that are used frequently develop stronger connections or "wiring"; and those that are rarely or never used eventually die and are pruned. By developing new connections and pruning away weak ones, the brain adapts to the changing environment. I like the phrase "Neural Darwinism" to describe this, which simply means survival of the busiest. Or, use it or lose it.

The brain goes through this synaptic pruning process daily, primarily during REM sleep, along with memory consolidation. This is a prime example of why we must be careful what we think about and dwell on; we become what we think about most of the time.

The good news is that if you're challenging and interrupting your negative and stressful thinking patterns, if you're being mindful and using the techniques in chapter eight and activating the relaxation response or other cognitive behavioral therapy techniques, you're rewiring in a self-directed way and interrupting the pattern. You can give yourself a pat on the back for that. You're not letting the rut get any deeper or negative pathways get any stronger. If those pathways have less energy and traffic directed towards them, then they will wither and eventually be pruned away. To return back to the string of lights analogy, the dimmest strings or networks will be pruned. The opposite of the stress of the fight or flight response is the relaxation response.

Next, we want to look at creating new (or strengthening existing) positive brain pathways or neural structure, self-directed neuroplasticity. We want to start thinking about how we'd like things to be, and how to get our brain more in sync with that and those strings brighter.

One disclaimer is that the change is incremental and not sudden or dramatic. There are a lot of oversimplified and misleading claims being made about the brain, as in, "Learn the secrets of how to rewire your brain and overcome PTSD or other traumas in a month." The creator of the brain-gaming company Lumosity paid a $2 million fine to settle charges from the Federal Trade Commission. The settlement alleged that Lumosity deceived customers with unfounded claims that its games could sharpen thinking in everyday life and protect against cognitive decline. Lumosity is still in business and now simply claims that its games are "designed by scientists to challenge core cognitive abilities." It's important to be realistic, but also not to dismiss that little efforts do add up over time. The brain is inherently lazy and doesn't want to make new connections unless forced to, so you need a lot of consistency, reinforcement, and to link rewards to your efforts.

Emotion plays a crucial role in rewiring. I have underestimated this over the years and not brought enough of it into my efforts to rewire. Emotion is the fuel, the juice, or the power behind creating new neural structure and bringing our intentions into reality. It's what leaves imprint on the brain. As the intensity of an experience increases, so do levels of the neurotransmitter norepinephrine, which promotes the formation of new synapses. If you open yourself up to the experience, enhance it, and it becomes more rewarding than your brain initially expected, dopamine levels also rise, which converts it into lasting neural structure.[26]

Remember the brain is faced with a deluge of information and sensory inputs. It's constantly deciding what's relevant and what can be ignored or pruned away. Without emotion a thought is neutral, it has no real power. In other words, it is not enough to engage in positive thinking or repeat positive affirmations if you are not feeling anything.

The longer something is held in awareness and the more emotionally stimulating it is, the more neurons fire and wire together, and the stronger the trace in memory. Our brains want us to recall the times we've been terrified so we won't repeat those circumstances. That's the obsolete prime directive of our brains; to keep us safe from physical danger. Fear and negative emotions leave quite an imprint on the brain. When you reflect on your frightening experiences, you realize why you remember them— because of the emotions you felt. Now we're doing the opposite; rewiring.

Due to its negativity bias, your brain prefers for you to be anxious, fearful and hypervigilant; that gives it a better chance of fulfilling its mission of keeping you alive and passing on your genes. With this negativity bias, negative experiences and what could go wrong are much more relevant to its mission. It's much more sensitive towards and interested in them. Finding negativity, watching out for and anticipating negativity, entertaining this, and replaying negativity. Negativity is given top priority.

Positive experiences? They're simply not as relevant. They're much easier and much more likely to be dismissed and ignored. They're not part of the brain's mission. An opportunity to connect intimately with someone to pass on the genes? Yes, the brain is interested in that, and releases oxytocin, or the love hormone, but that's an exception to its usual dismissal of positive experiences. This is why bad news and sex sells.

Have you ever seen a news teaser promoting a lead story of positive news? It's usually something similar to, "Eating this food can kill you. Find out what it is at 11 p.m." This is also why, as Dr. Rick Hanson puts it so well, our brains are "like Velcro for negative experiences and Teflon for positive ones."

Due to all this, which of your neural networks, positive or negative, do you think is stronger and has more activity or traffic? If you guessed the negative ones, you're right. The mind is like a garden, but the soil is much more conducive to growing the negative weeds. It becomes a vicious cycle. Since these negative neural networks are stronger, it means they react faster, are more in tune with, are looking for, and see the negative events in our lives as more relevant, important, and worthy of careful analysis. All this perpetuates more of a bias towards the negative since we always find what we're looking for. We not only see fewer positive events; the ones we do recognize are determined to be less relevant and are easily discounted.

This means we have to work at it. We must make a concerted effort to balance out this negativity bias— to even the playing field. Think of your playing field and ask yourself if it needs to be evened out. Ask yourself what percentage of the time you estimate that you think negatively and reinforce those neural pathways, and what percentage of the time you think about the positive things and experiences in your life and reinforce those neural pathways?

To balance this out, it's vital that we start paying more attention to and savoring our everyday positive experiences. I don't mean positive thinking; I mean positive experiences. It's the little things that are easy to discount. We all have several, if not many, of these throughout our day, but it's easy to quickly move on from them since our brains don't find them as relevant. In Rick Hanson's excellent book *Hardwired for Happiness*, he champions savoring and its benefits, which is compelling. The recommendation is to hold the positive experience in your awareness for at least 10 seconds, a reasonable amount of time, instead of quickly discounting it.

Savoring is good for you in so many ways, to include just making you an overall happier person. In fact, researchers have demonstrated that the very act of imagining a pleasurable scene or recollecting a positive emotion rapidly provokes a transition of heart rate variability toward a phase of coherence. The term 'coherence' is used by scientists to describe a highly efficient physiological state in which the cardiovascular, nervous, hormonal and immune systems are all working efficiently and harmoniously. Coherence in heart rhythm by savoring affects the brain's limbic system, fostering stability and signaling that everything is in working order physiologically. The limbic system then reacts to this message by reinforcing coherence in the heart. [27]

The longer something is held in awareness and the more emotionally stimulating it is, the more neurons you get firing and wiring together. You also get a stronger trace in memory, and this creates more neural structure over time. The definition of savoring is to "taste, enjoy, or relish." That's exactly what we should be doing for at least 10 seconds. As I'm experiencing a nice moment, I will usually hold a smile for 10 seconds. If for some reason it's not a good time or place to smile, I'll attempt to smile internally. I do this by envisioning something as simple as the sun shining, my kids excitedly playing together, or making plans for the day.

Smiling has multiple kinds of positive effects on us. Forcing a fake smile provides the same benefits. When you smile, the brain senses the muscle activity and assumes humor and good things are happening. The feel-good neurotransmitters— dopamine, endorphins and serotonin— are all released when a smile flashes across your face. This not only relaxes your body, it can also lower your heart rate and blood pressure. In a sense, the brain is a sucker for a grin. It doesn't bother to sort out whether you're smiling because you're genuinely joyous or just pretending.

We can train the brain to revel in the positive. Noticing when things are good and making an effort to soak that in feeds dopamine— a positive neurotransmitter— to our amygdala, helping it to want and seek out more dopamine. This also causes the amygdala to call for less cortisol, which is a monumental development. Soaking up the good builds a reservoir of happiness for when things get bad. Some researchers say we need to have a ratio of three positive experiences for every one negative experience to enhance our resiliency and be able to bounce back from adversity. Your adversity quotient is a key part of life.

What we need to do is be hypervigilant for fulfilling experiences that happen. When we experience favorable outcomes, we must try to enhance it, absorb it, and really let the feeling sink down into us. I like to remind myself that, "This is a good moment, right here, right now. I want to stay with this moment, to enhance it, and remember it— to get me more oriented towards seeing more and finding more good moments. To get those circuits nice and well-traveled in my brain." I don't care if people see me smiling.

Even if you've been diagnosed with moderate or severe depression, there should still be several positive experiences that you're exposed to each day— unless you're somehow a prisoner or being subjected to torture. Ask yourself which positive emotion you're feeling. Also, what about the experience makes you feel this way?

Here's a list of common positive emotions to be on the lookout for and enhance:

| | | |
|---|---|---|
| confidence | love | inspiration |
| admiration | elation | awe |
| appreciation | exhilaration | elevation |
| enthusiasm | brightness | altruism |
| excitement | pleasure | satisfaction |
| engagement | contentment | relief |
| eagerness | appreciation | affection |
| euphoria | engaged | cheerfulness |
| contentment | uplifted | surprise |
| peaceful | motivated | joy |
| comforted | enthusiasm | gratitude |
| enjoyment | hopeful | serenity |
| optimism | pride | interest |
| happiness | amusement | thankfulness |

I was pleasantly surprised to see a similar list on a sign outside the entry door of my youngest child's grammar school. The sign urges students to be:

| | | |
|---|---|---|
| helpful | strong | savvy |
| honest | social | charismatic |
| different | patient | accepting |
| fun | happy | punctual |
| honest | supportive | exceptional |

| polite | creative | unique |
| playful | open | authentic |
| reliable | friendly | responsible |
| yourself | consistent | flexible |
| reachable | imperfect | determined |
| amazing | cooperative | remarkable |
| true | caring | charming |
| memorable | creative | dedicated |
| bold | organized | |

These are all things that we want to grow in our experience. Rewiring efforts work like compound interest. The more you feel these emotions and enhance these experiences, the more of the experiences you'll find, as it becomes a positive self-perpetuating cycle.

If you think about it, aren't positive experiences what we're really after in life? The pursuit of happiness is mentioned as a fundamental right in the Declaration of Independence. Isn't the purpose of the pursuit to feel the emotion of happiness? What good is having an experience but not feeling any joy or satisfaction in it? We want the emotional experience. It's what drives us. In performance psychology and sales, it's common knowledge that human beings don't stretch themselves and sacrifice for logic-based, surface-level motivators. It's always the deeper emotions that drive us. It's not the steak, it's the sizzle of the steak.

We must give ourselves— and allow— these experiences. People may say, "I want to win the lottery." But why? So they don't have to worry about money anymore? If that's the case, isn't what they really want a feeling of contentment, safety, and an absence of worry? Then make the effort to feel those emotions and have that experience (As an aside, surveys have shown a year after winning the lottery, levels of satisfaction and contentment decrease). Then you attract more contentment and safety in your life. We think we want things, but we really want the experiences that we think those things will provide us.

The bad news is that winning the lottery won't necessarily make you happy. The good news is you don't need to win the lottery to be happy. Many people also think they'll be happy once they are successful or that success brings happiness. Success comes from happiness. It's the fuel for success.

The other thing we need to be doing is to go on the offense, mentally. This is paramount since we know the default state of our brains is to be in defense mode, to prepare for the danger and threats it believes we're surrounded by and will be hit with imminently. But ask yourself, how often are you on the offense? Or do you remain in the default and mostly think about what you don't want, or fear will happen? Do you ever spend time thinking about what you do want or how you'd like things to be? Imagine if you were to suddenly stop people and ask them, "What are you thinking about right now?" and get an honest answer. The most successful, or the top 10% of income earners, are thinking about what they want and how they're going to get it.

Here are some revealing self-discovery questions for you to fill in the answer to. In the boxes below, write down how frequently, or what percentage of the time, you estimate you think about:

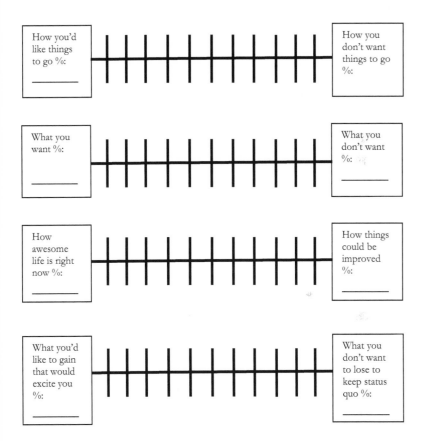

| How you'd like things to go %: | | How you don't want things to go %: |
| What you want %: | | What you don't want %: |
| How awesome life is right now %: | | How things could be improved %: |
| What you'd like to gain that would excite you %: | | What you don't want to lose to keep status quo %: |

We've all heard the phrase, "Be careful what you wish for." It might be more effective to say, "Be careful what you give your energy and attention to." Are you familiar with the popular book and movie, *The Secret?* It states, "If you are looking for the love of your life, stop;

when you start doing things you love he or she will be waiting for you." This has truth to it, but it has received some criticism, which I think is justified, about not emphasizing enough the action pieces that people must also take. Intentions are good, but your actions must meet your intentions. You can visualize being thin, but if there is dissonance in your actions and you eat poorly you won't meet your goals.

However, the Law of Attraction is fascinating and has been studied and proven repeatedly. For example, if you repeatedly and effectively visualize yourself at your ideal weight and feel the positive emotions that go along with that, according to the law your brain will take that as an instruction and create those circumstances and you will instinctually stop yourself from eating poorly.

We attract into our lives the circumstances that coincide with our dominant thoughts and feelings. Most of us spend way too much energy on what we don't want, which just gives us more of the experience of what we don't want. When you grasp that what you focus on you will get, you become very careful of what you focus on. This is why Mother Teresa said, "I was once asked why I don't participate in anti-war demonstrations. I said that I will never do that, but as soon as you have a pro-peace rally, I'll be there." She didn't want to give her energy to opposing war. It must be about peace.

Negativity, or being in opposition, clashes with the law of attraction. For example, having a goal of getting out of debt will always keep you in debt. It must be about prosperity.

We also have to be careful of how we describe ourselves. Too often when we make sweeping generalizations about our lives, we make all of the negative things come true— whether we want to or not. It's not helpful when people say something like, 'I'm a constant worrier," since just making the statement reinforces it. It's better to say, "I'm getting better every day thinking about what I want to have happen."

We do this programming work by visualizing what we'd like to manifest or have happen in our lives and savoring it as though we've already achieved it.

## Create a Video

The best way to get going with this and getting on the offense is to create a video. We're all very familiar with this medium due to all the electronics and viral clips that we're viewing. If I let them, my kids could easily watch YouTube videos all day. Back before we had all these screens, radio was our entertainment. Radio was known as the theater of the mind since we were forced to picture what was being described to us. The Halloween 1938 "War of the Worlds" broadcast by Orson Welles is a great example.

Creating our own mental images is a skill that we're losing since it's all done for us. Very few people do it, and we need to get better at it. When are we forced to imagine? This is critical because if we can imagine it, we can create it. That's what the research tells us. Worry is really a misuse of imagination since we're previewing exactly what we don't want. I like to break the word imagine in half, as in "image-in." Albert Einstein told us that "Imagination is everything. It is the preview of life's coming attractions." Since our outer worlds really are a reflection of our inner worlds, it's vital to invest time imaging in what we want. More than a static visualization, this programs your neural circuitry step-by-step, so that when you begin the action steps, you have already created the path or highway for neurons to travel so you can rapidly achieve your goals.

To create your video, go to a place where you won't be distracted. Avoid attempting this when you're rushed or tense. The brain is more amenable to this type of programming when it is slowed down; perhaps in the morning or after you've meditated. Start by getting a clear mental picture of the end result you'd like to achieve. Then get a clear mental picture of yourself going through all the steps leading to that end result, as though you were watching someone else on a screen. See it in as much detail as you possibly can. Where are you, what exactly are you doing and saying, and how are you doing it and saying it? Who else is there, and what are the others doing and saying?

Repeatedly replay your mental video and sharpen the images each time. The brain also has novelty bias so try to make it new and somewhat different each time you replay this video. Perhaps experience it from a different angle, which will help immersion in the brain. The more clearly you can see your video, the more motivation it will give you. Tony Robbins says, "There's no such thing as unmotivated people, just people who don't have goals that excite them." As you're creating and viewing your video, keep asking yourself what excites you, really pumps you up, and gives you a sense of accomplishment. Feel those emotions that connect with your end result: enhance them, absorb them, and really savor the entire experience by letting the feeling sink into you. Just like when you recall a past negative, stressful, or fearful experience, your brain can't tell the time difference. Along with your body, your brain relives the experience each time you replay it.

If that sounds too abstract, it's not. Our limbic brain system that feels emotions is unable to distinguish between things we're thinking about and currently experiencing in reality. When you're mentally rehearsing your new habits or what you want to image in, you strengthen your ability to create them in your life. It's almost like you've created a good memory, but you're really creating instructions for your brain to follow.

One potential pitfall is that if you don't believe it's possible, you're going to have a hard time imagining a desired goal. Wayne Dyer wrote a book on this entitled, *You'll See it When You Believe it.* You may have to do a frank reassessment of your beliefs and work on first believing it's possible and that you deserve it. Seeing is not required for believing; but skeptical people may say they'll only believe it when they see it. Some people hold themselves back if they feel undeserving. We only allow ourselves the levels of success that align with our self-concept. Self-sabotage is real. You may have to delve deeper into this. Some good resources would be *Self Esteem: The Ultimate program for self-help* by Matthew McKay and Patrick Fanning, and *Self Esteem: Simple*

*Steps to Build Your Confidence* by Gael Lindenfield.

Your videos aren't restricted to major life changes; they could be something as basic as acting more confidently at work. You could mirror or emulate someone who you feel is a confident leader. "Fake it till you make it" really does work. You can simply develop a clear mental video of yourself acting in a highly self-assured manner in job situations, much like your role model or ideal leader might act. You could also imagine that a director of a television series has cast you, as an actor, to play the role of a confident manager that people respect. You'd be unconcerned about other people since you've been told the camera will be focused on you alone. The director just wants you to adopt professional mannerisms and have you speak and act with superior self-confidence. Above all, your face must exude confidence and express no self-doubt. You should appear as though things are going exactly the way you'd like them to and you're getting the results you want. Resolve to act exactly like this for four full days, as if you were a character in a play. Continue to replay your mind video between acts of your play. All of the studies and research show that people feel more confident after pretending they were confident.

You could have a more specific end result. A ready example is from the sales industry. How would you define success in sales? When a customer signs a contract or purchase order? See that happening and feel the emotions that go along with it. Ellen DeGeneres likes to tell the story of how she clearly visualized doing a smashing stand-up routine on *The Tonight Show* and Johnny Carson inviting her to sit down on his couch afterwards. Getting an offer to sit on the couch after your performance instantly changed the lives of stand-up comedians. She kept replaying this video for a few years and in 1986 it came true, and she was the first woman in the history of the show to be called over to sit down. Before he was famous, comedian Jim Carey wrote himself a check for $10,000,000 for "acting services rendered" and post-dated it three years later. He kept the check in his wallet and would park his car on the famous Mulholland Drive every night and visualize having directors interested in him and people he respected saying, "I like your work." Just before Thanksgiving 1995, Jim Carey found out he would be receiving $10,000,000 for his role in *Dumb and Dumber.*

Successful athletes regularly do this to achieve great results, and you can do the same thing. A baseball hitter may clearly see the pitcher release the ball, swinging with great mechanics, the bat hitting the ball, the flight of the ball going over the fence, see himself rounding the bases, the awesome feeling of hitting a home run, the roar of the crowd, and the emotional reactions from his teammates as he returns to the dugout. When was the last time you envisioned a home run scene like that? Probably never, unless baseball is important to you and hitting a home run is a goal of yours.

A vision board is another tool many people have had success with. It's any sort of board on which you display images or words that represent whatever you want to be, do or have in your life. It's helpful to clarify, concentrate and maintain focus on a specific life goal along with serving as inspiration and motivation.

Without emotion, thoughts or images are neutral and have no real power. It's not enough to just play your video or repeat positive affirmations if you're not feeling anything. If you're struggling with this, ask yourself which emotion(s) from the prior of positive emotions you would like to feel. Then ask yourself, for example, "What does exhilarated feel like? Then, start to feel it. You can ask yourself, "What would someone who's exhilarated breathe like and what would his facial expressions look like?" Then you can start to mirror those. You can also recall a prior time when you felt exhilarated and try to link those emotions to what you'd currently like to image in. It's also helpful if you choose a word or phrase that's associated with the feelings you want to experience, then when you reach your ideal state say this cue word to yourself over and over to create an association between the cue word and the ideal state. With practice, saying this cue word or phrase to yourself can make it easier to reconnect to your ideal positive state.

If it's difficult to envision what you'd like to image in or manifest in your life, just ask yourself what you don't want, or what's been causing you angst or anxiety. Sometimes the negatives and avoiding harms can be a powerful motivator. Then you just create a video of the exact opposite. Good questions to ask yourself are, "How would I like to feel?" and "Would I rather be right or happy?" I have a friend who's been worried about his marriage. He'd have a fight with his wife and then quickly jump to how difficult it was going to be to create an online dating profile and re-enter the dating pool after so many years. The question always has to be, "Is that what you'd like to have happen?" It wasn't, so his video clearly showed him and his spouse feeling connected and both saying that they loved each other. The emotions he held during the playing of the video were gratitude and joy.

"Expect the best and prepare for the worst" is a reasonable philosophy to live by at times, as long as you're not imaging the worst or what you don't want to a counter-productive extent. It's not negative to have contingency plans and prepare for various things that could go wrong. After all, the Boy Scout motto is, "Be prepared." Dwight Eisenhower, the former president and commander of the D-Day invasion, spent one-year strategizing and planning for the invasion. He was once asked about the scenario of the invading troops being beaten back at the beaches. He replied, "That would have been bad, but I never allowed my mind to think that way."

Affirmations also help, along with writing yourself a positive anchor script. This is an internal monologue that bolsters your self-image. It's like a personal mission statement that you review frequently. These type of statements and affirmations must be both personal and positive. It doesn't work to say 'I'm not stressed' since there is a negative in the statement. They also must be in the present tense, as if it's already so. An affirmation can be as simple as, "I'm enjoying a healthy height to weight proportion." The subconscious mind has no choice but to accept what it hears.

We're too focused on weaknesses that could be improved. That energy would be better served accentuating strengths. To showcase these, ask yourself the following three questions: "I am at my best when _____; When I'm at my best I am _____; When I'm at my best I do _____." The idea is to see yourself through three different lenses. An example could be, "I am at my best when I am working on things which inspire, inform and excite others."

Our minds are never still. It's easy to let negative messages drift through our minds and take over. Have many of these positive statements ready and review them or play them frequently. Here's a longer example of a positive anchor script:

*"I have tons of energy, talent, and enthusiasm. I'm a dedicated and hard worker. People are drawn to me, find me likeable, and I'm awesome at making sales. My customers value my insights and our products, want to hear from me, and are loyal to me. I am the best sales rep in our region and my sales are consistently going up. This is getting me noticed, making me proud, and bringing more money into my family. I'm doing it. It's happening. I believe in myself, this company and my team. I know I'm making a difference— today and every day."*

Keep reminding yourself that you become what you think and feel most of the time, so keep coming back to these types of emotions and videos. Consciously practice thinking, feeling, visualizing and acting in alignment with your desired intention. When you do this, you will stop the unconscious habit of recycling the past and activate your ability to rewire your brain in the present moment. Just keep repeating and replaying. If you do this repeatedly for a few weeks, you'll probably only need to repeat it when things seem tough or stressful.

# 12. Entrenched Negativity

Sometimes it's more effective to engage and remove what's negative before attempting to instill the positive and rewire. Pulling out the weeds first can make rewiring and planting new networks easier. Especially for those of us who have had experiences that were disruptive or traumatic, there will be continuing consequences if they are not confronted. Long-standing emotional baggage from the past can easily affect us today. Negative or anxiety-producing patterns can easily keep replaying; they form a deeper rut and stronger network connections each time they play in a self-perpetuating cycle.

Some people don't want to review the past. It can be painful, scary and unsettling. There must be a middle ground between these following two extremes:

1/ The past has nothing to do with my present or future. What happened back then doesn't matter; what matters is today.

2/ The victim mindset, as in, "Look where I came from or what happened to me; there is nothing I can do to get past it." The trends of generational poverty and the inheritance of mindsets and other issues demonstrate this.

If we want to change our brains and remove negative patterns, it's important to take an objective look back at what happened to us and consider how it may affect us today.

Specifically, how disruptive, negative, or traumatic experiences can:

- create negative emotions and coping mechanisms

- affect our beliefs, especially our self-limiting beliefs

- affect our ability to navigate our noise

- affect our ability to deal with automatic negative thoughts

- affect our ability to have an accurate self-concept

- affect our ability to rewire our brain

We've all had pain, setbacks, and unwanted changes thrust upon us. It's important to ask what might have happened in your life that could have instilled negative patterns. What scared you, overwhelmed you, or caused you to feel bad about yourself? What didn't you know how to process or understand?

Many of us had a stable upbringing, in a stable household with two parents whom we felt loved us. Some of us never had that. If you had it, that gives you a solid start in life, a firm foundation, self-confidence, and a better development without fear.

Many of us tend to downplay and minimize traumas and disruptions that happened, especially during childhood when we're most vulnerable. Something that might not seem like a big deal to an adult can be a significant event in children's lives based on when it happened to them and how they were equipped to deal with it at that time. Something as innocent as a child falling off an elevated play area and suffering an injury can leave a lasting trace. A lot of kids ask, "What's wrong with me, why did I fall?" They end up blaming themselves and creating a painful memory that has aftereffects. There is quite a spectrum of trauma, and everyone's experiences of trauma are personal. Every individual and situation is unique. Dealing with a car accident can range from a minor inconvenience for some to a life-altering experience of horror for others.

It's important to objectively recall all of the details that you may gloss over or discount. The details of what happened gives you insights. You might say, "Of course I've felt _____. Anyone who went through that would." These are valuable awarenesses, especially since our brains are pre-programmed to focus on doom and gloom. When did the doom and gloom start? When did I first experience that?

It's also important to consider how other people related to you, and how they made you feel during this time when you were beginning to form your self-concept. We all have core beliefs, or schemas, about our self-worth and the world around us. This drives our automatic thoughts, our relationships, how loveable and successful we feel we are. These all get formed in childhood. Anything that may have affected how you see yourself is especially important to consider examining.

Here is what I recollected after asking myself these questions:

I came from a large middle-class family of seven children, and I was the youngest child. My oldest sibling is 15 years older than I and the next closest to me in age is six years older. I was quite a surprise as my parents never expected another child.

My earliest memories from childhood were happy with lots of activity going on in our large Victorian house, which my parents had bought well before I was born. When I was very young, I'm sure I was a novelty, and fun for my siblings to play with. When I was five, my siblings were 20, 18, 16, 15 and 11. I remember being in kindergarten at the same elementary school that my sixth-grade brother was in, and it was exciting to see him outside at recess and walking home in the same line. The next year, he was gone. I didn't know my two oldest brothers very well since they either moved out or were in college before I was old enough to remember anything.

By the time I was 10 and they were 25, 23, 21, 20 and 16, things were changed significantly. It was almost as if I was an only child. Most of my siblings had left and the activity in the house dwindled. I can remember a sense of loss from this as in, "Where did everyone go?" In retrospect, if I were simply an only child from the start, it wouldn't have felt like abandonment.

Some other dark clouds arrived. My 19-year-old brother was hospitalized for five months (in those times they kept you as an inpatient for a long time) with a major mental illness. I can remember him coming home for visits and crawling on all fours like an infant. To this day, I still coordinate most of his needs. My 16-year-old brother was involved with drugs and lived in a foster home. He also petitioned to legally change his last name. I guess he was embarrassed.

This created a tension and atmosphere of adult problems in our home. The playfulness and childhood security were gone. My mother, perhaps going through menopause, was very emotional and seemed to be bitter and aggrieved. Maybe she was at the end of her rope. She had five children under the age of five at one point. There was always a conflict or drama underway.

One family Thanksgiving was ruined because of a fight between my mother, grandmother and great-aunt over where I was going to sit. My grandmother and sister became angry and left in a taxi. For years, no one spoke to each other. We would attend family counseling where we were observed through one-way windows.

When I was 12, my father also left the house. He was always calmer and easier to relate to, but the night he left was an ugly scene. My parents were in a raucous fight where the police responded. Things were building up for a long time, and my father just snapped. My parents wrestled on the floor; my father was holding my mother down. I was rocking back and forth sobbing in the corner of the room, holding a large steak knife when the police arrived. I'm not sure what I thought I was doing with the knife, but I know I was terrified with this traumatic scene and watching the rest of my carefree childhood shatter.

The next day, my father came to gather his belongings. I was under strict orders to not let him in the house and I turned him away. It was not healthy for me to be put in the middle like that. My mother obtained a temporary order for custody and child support until the divorce was final. Now the big house consisted of my mother and me.

My parents' divorce affected me more than my siblings since they were already college age or older. I was the one who was stuck at home and bore the brunt of the impact. My mom began renting out some of the empty bedrooms in our house to college students, which seemed so odd and almost like a violation to me. Eventually, during high school I moved in with my father in his small apartment.

I realize that these events did not give me a solid or stable foundation to build on through my adolescent years. I was quiet, shy and lacked self-esteem. With all the upheaval and people that had left, or I felt abandoned by, I think on some level I had the mindset of, "There must be something wrong with me." This was not helpful. Nor is it something that most young people would be aware of or express unless an effort is made to probe what's going on with them.

I was a Christmas baby, a year younger than my peers, was skinny, didn't play sports, or have many friends. In school I was bullied and was once stuffed into a locker by some older kids. This was decades before the anti-bullying movement.

These adverse events reinforced the negative mindset that there must be something wrong with me. This can easily create a belief system and immersion in confirmation bias, where you keep finding more evidence that confirms your beliefs and discard evidence that runs counter to your beliefs. Once the brain believes something, it starts collecting the evidence to back it up and attracts more of the same. It's hard for some of us to consider views that oppose our own and that challenge our worldview. Almost as if the brain is saying, "You see, here's exhibit number one, and here is exhibit number two!" The brain also starts preparing for the doom and gloom. But a belief is just a set of thoughts that we've been holding and believing for a long time. The preparing, bracing and collecting of evidence are not helpful; it's much better to work on changing the belief.

I don't recall receiving much help in planning my future. I enlisted in the Army and left for basic training a month after my high school graduation. That was good for me, gave me confidence, and getting away from my hometown and all the issues there was healthy. Upon discharge, I worked in the radiology profession, went to college at night, and continued a typical path through life.

That's my backstory. I hope I don't sound like a victim; I'm not. Many have endured more challenging circumstances and obstacles. I was never abused or had anything similarly dramatic happen. I didn't dwell in my past or consider it that significant; I just went on living my life the best I could.

Whatever pain we've endured, there's a common tendency to ignore heartache, loss or traumas, especially with men. It's easy to say just get over it, or that's in the past. Time, of course, doesn't heal all wounds. Physical wounds perhaps, but not emotional wounds, especially during your formative years. Post-traumatic stress disorder (PTSD) can occur at any age, even from dealing with a toxic boss.

Externally, my childhood affected my ability to develop healthy relationships. I was most likely bracing myself in anticipation of someone leaving or I felt unworthy of them; classic abandonment anxiety. I was also deficient in having fun and enjoying myself.

Consequently, I'm more interested in the internal since that's where we must look to heal it. How did these disruptive or traumatic events affect my brain? This is crucial because, when we endure a disruptive or traumatic event, our brain struggles to process and digest what happened.

When a traumatic event happens, the level of the neurotransmitter's norepinephrine and epinephrine in the brain encodes memories into the hippocampus. With all this brain activity, traumatic memories are not stored in the brain the same way as regular activity. Instead, trauma splits off, or is "locked" in the brain while other details fade.[28]

That's why survivors of traumatic assault can vividly remember events, regardless of the time lapsed. Post-traumatic effects of an event like this are long-lasting. The hippocampus shrinks when a person has PTSD, which indicates that the hippocampus isn't functioning the way it should. Often, this can lead to vivid or specific flashbacks of the event.[29]

Our brain isn't able to absorb what overwhelms it. It doesn't know how and where to file things. Since things can't be processed by the brain, the brain is stuck frozen. It's not able to move past it or heal.

Was my brain stuck on my disruptive, traumatic events? Although they weren't as dramatic as what many have endured, I think the answer is yes. Even more than the usual negativity bias, my brain was predisposed to prepare for more bad news. It wasn't pondering or preparing for the next victorious thing that I'd like to see. My brain was biased towards setbacks. Anticipating and ruminating on what can go wrong is counterproductive. The notion that dark clouds are imminent can be changed. You're in control of this.

Talking things over with someone who validates is helpful; we're only as sick as our secrets. This is why support groups are so effective.

It's even better to go deeper to heal the brain— to reprocess or desensitize yourself to disruptive or traumatic memories that your brain has not been able to successfully digest and file away.

One of the best ways to accomplish this is EMDR, or eye movement desensitization and reprocessing. It was first introduced in the late 1980s, and I had first heard about it around 20 years ago. I wished I had done it sooner and found it to be very helpful. EMDR initially had its fair share of skeptics, but today, this therapy, which has been the subject of many research studies, has become more widely accepted for use in the treatment of mental health, especially trauma diagnoses.

More than 30 randomized clinical trials have shown EMDR to be effective for PTSD. The American Psychiatric Association, the Veterans Administration Department of Defense (VA-DOD) and other national and international practice guidelines have approved EMDR as a Level A treatment for PTSD. One study, funded by the HMO Kaiser Permanente, found that 100% of the single-trauma victims and 77% of multiple trauma victims no longer were diagnosed with PTSD after only six 50-minute sessions. In another study, 77% of combat veterans were free of PTSD in 12 sessions.

Since many symptoms of other mental health illnesses are based on adverse life experiences, EMDR also helps to alleviate many other conditions in addition to trauma. Everyday memories and accumulations of small events may cause us to have low self-esteem or prevent us from believing we deserve the best.

In EMDR, you essentially rewrite memories of damaging life experiences and take your power back. The old wounds just don't have the same emotional hold over you. It's as though you remember things now more in black and white than vivid color— with all its accompanying, unsettling details. It won't be as upsetting or scary the next time you remember or visualize that picture.

The eye movement part of this practice is now downplayed. "It's really about bilateral stimulation of both hemispheres of the brain, and there are several other effective ways to do this, such as tapping, sound, or vibration," says Sharon Schwartz, a prominent practitioner and speaker on EMDR. It's recommended you do this with a trained therapist to facilitate the process. It involves recalling the painful experiences while simultaneously doing bilateral stimulation. I've seen people simply passing a ball back and forth between their hands and watching the movement closely while recalling a memory.

The brain is extremely complicated, and it's hard to definitively say how EMDR works. Most researchers and psychologists surmise that performing two tasks simultaneously, e.g., recalling a memory and doing bilateral stimulation at the same time, requires working memory capacity and interferes with working memory processes. This leaves less room for the unwanted memory, thus making it less vivid and less emotional.

This is reasonable since it's virtually impossible to pay attention to two things at the same time. By switching gears quickly, you shift the arousal state. People with trauma can be stuck and have trouble switching gears. The memories will always be there, but with EMDR you have practice with accessing, being exposed to those moments, and making them less powerful. This helps to train the amygdala since it only learns from experience; you can't use reasoning or logic to tackle anxiety that arises from reactions in the amygdala itself, as opposed from thoughts in the cortex. This type of exposure therapy is a form of rewiring, as it helps the amygdala "unlearn" associations between danger and particular experiences, like authority figures, loud voices or driving a car, etc. Gradual, repeated exposure to whatever's causing anxiety is a way to help the amygdala learn a more neutral association between the experience and our reaction to it. EMDR also gets beneath our inherent resistance to being exposed to the memory or things that run counter to our pre-held beliefs.

Another theory is that EMDR facilitates access to adaptive memory, similar to the REM phase of sleep, when the brain processes the day's residue and files it away. Disturbing life events or memories seem to be stored in a fragmented form. Most of our memories and negative material is not reopened and activated in the same way you would reopen a document on a computer. It's not retrieved as a whole, but rather reconstructed very quickly by the brain in an active process in which vast numbers of synapses take fractions of a second to sync up together into a kind of confederation that represents the experience of the materials.

EMDR appears to facilitate the reconnections of these fragments. The brain knows where it needs to go to make the neural connections for healing to occur and it does this work. This is how EMDR seems to allow for adaptive resolution of disturbing life events, a shift from negative to positive cognitions about them, and to effectively *resolve* these adverse life experiences and any hold they have over you.

Hypnosis is another tool that many find helpful in dealing with entrenched negativity. Suspended disbelief addresses experiences that are stored in the subconscious and gets through the conscious resistance. It can help you connect ideas to feelings and to other concepts. You can use hypnosis to connect harmful thoughts to concepts like "not allowed" or "bad consequences," or even "I would never do that." Hypnosis can also help to express and dissipate stored emotions that are connected to past disruptive events and thoughts.

One simple hypnosis example is the "swish" technique. You picture the negative thought as vividly as you can onto a television screen and gauge its emotional impact. Then think of a good thought and put it in the corner, like picture-in-picture. Then slowly "swish" the two so the good thought occupies the screen, and the bad one disappears. Do this over and over for several minutes at a time. Your goal is this: The next time the original trigger image appears or when the negative thought pops in your mind, it should be diminished, almost as if the thought has been replaced. There are a wide variety of hypnotherapy practitioners who can guide you through different aspects of the practice, depending on what you'd like to accomplish.

One hypnotherapist I know is very successful in convincing patients' subconscious that they have had stomach stapling surgery, and their stomachs are significantly smaller. They therefore eat less and meet their weight-loss goals. The subconscious has no choice but to accept what we tell it, even if we consciously don't believe it.

There are many possibilities and different approaches available to remove entrenched negativity from your brain if you believe it's possible, suspend disbelief, and give it a chance.

# 13. Other People

A large part of mental toughness revolves around other people. We can't live with people and we can't live without them. We expend a lot of our mental energy focused on other people; much of this is wasted energy. Human beings are the ultimate social species. Satisfying relationships mean everything in life. They provide most of our joy in life, as opposed to drawing from our own accomplishments. Researchers have found pronoun use to be reliable in identifying depression since people with symptoms of depression use significantly more first-person singular pronouns— such as "me", "myself" and "I"— and far less second- and third- person pronouns— such as "they", "them" or "she". This suggests people with depression are more focused on themselves, and less connected with others. Loneliness not only kills people effectively; people don't talk about it.

But other people can drive us crazy if we let them. We are vulnerable to poor human interaction. What can we do to minimize this? It's understandable to feel devastated when things fall apart with your significant other or close family members. My focus is people in the periphery of our lives— work colleagues, friends, acquaintances, extended relatives, etc. We give them too much of ourselves— our mental space and peace of mind. As Sally Kempton says, "It's hard to fight an enemy who has outposts in your head." So many of us give so much free or low-cost rent in our head to others! We've got to make it much more difficult to gain a foothold there. Ask yourself, "What is my rental rate?"

Look at the image below. Imagine these two people had a difficult interaction. What's more important is after the fact— How easily do you give up space in your head? The person on the right is coming out way ahead here.

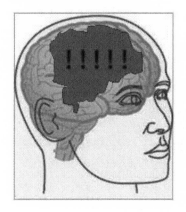 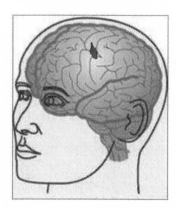

## We're powerless over them

There are a few things we need to remind ourselves regarding others. First, we don't have control over people. We're powerless over them. To admit this takes a lot of pressure off. We can't magically get people to change or conform to our wishes and be the way we'd like them to be. We don't need to feel guilty about it, as if it's a failure on our part. If you have a personal or professional relationship with someone, hopefully you have some influence over them, and they should care about how you see things. If the relationship is important enough to both parties, enough effort should be made on both sides to communicate, compromise and adjust. But not always. It takes two.

You can't compel someone to engage and have an effective dialogue with you. Some people don't want to truly listen and learn about your perspective. Some people's concept of a dialogue is actually a monologue that they expect you to agree with unconditionally. Compromise means you have to give something up. Both sides must find a middle ground. Some people will say they are willing to since it sounds good, but they're not.

One thing that we should be insisting on is that everyone's entitled to her own viewpoints, but not her own facts. You can see things differently and have different interpretations than others. You can agree to disagree on how you see things. But there's no one who's been given the Sacred Truth Scrolls whose interpretation is 100% correct.

We can't make others reciprocate the same feelings we have for them. Some people we love don't have the ability to love us back. They don't have any love to give.

We've had playmates of our kids with parents who we liked and seemed like it would be a great match for the families to hang out and spend time with. But it doesn't always work; we can't be the only ones reaching out and trying if they won't reciprocate. On the flip side, we've had parents who we get along well with, but the kids don't. Some people just won't like us, for whatever arbitrary reason. Maybe we remind them of someone else or share a first name with someone who was mean to them. We must accept this— for our own health and sanity. I'm not saying it's not disappointing. Sometimes you have to use the old sales catchphrase, "Some will, some won't, so what; next!

As Byron Katie tells us, "It's not your job to like me. It's mine." The less needy and high maintenance we are, the better.

## We don't know the full story

People are complicated, and we don't know the full story of what's going on with them. We don't know why they do what they do or think the way they think. We can guess what's happening with our theories and stories, but we usually don't have all the facts. It's good to remind yourself that not everyone thinks the same way you do. Everyone has a separate reality system. Whatever they do, or however they think, is because it makes sense for them within their reality system. It may not make sense to us. It may be self-destructive on their part. It may not be objective reality or based on facts. But, we must tell ourselves it is what it is.

Everyone's dealing with something. They're dealing with their own issues that we're not aware of. It may be obvious that they need help, but not everyone wants help or can be helped. They may not have the capacity to meet our needs. No one is perfect and can meet all our needs. If you expect that, you're just setting yourself up for disappointment and heartache. Some people can't love us back the way we need or don't speak the same love language. We must have our non-negotiables and "nice to have" lists. I'm not saying it's not sad and frustrating, but we can't exacerbate the problem by allowing them a large beachhead in our heads.

The people who annoy us the most can be our greatest teachers about what's going on with us. Ask yourself, "What about them or their behavior triggers something in me?" It's our judging of others that creates problems. It's so easy to do because they're right in front of us. Earl Nightingale told us, "When you judge others, you don't define them, you define yourself." I'd add to that: When you judge others, you create too much mental noise and give them too much headspace.

It's healthy to acknowledge that people can be exasperating and infuriating. It's also healthy to acknowledge that sometimes we need to work on ourselves and not be so sensitive and bothered by others. How easily offended you are is a significant statement about you and your ability to have a peaceful mind. Marcus Aurelius told us, "Choose not to be harmed and you won't feel harmed. Don't feel harmed and you haven't been."

It's better to give people the benefit of the doubt. The number of people who either get injured, sustain property damage, or legal trouble from road rage incidents is insane. Those people are generally strangers who we've never met before and will never see again. Few people have the intention of wanting to ruin our day. If someone is driving erratically, maybe we can assume they're going to the hospital or having a crisis. Or maybe we'll take it personally and get angry.

We need to focus on not letting them in so much. We need a firewall around us so people's behavior and issues bounce off. Focus more on yourself and what you need to do to take care of yourself so you can perform at your best.

A common refrain is, "I can't understand how they can be that way." No, you can't. So stop trying. It accomplishes nothing but to infuriate you and make you feel insane. You can't understand the understandable. You can't explain the unexplainable. You can't reason with the unreasonable. Who knows why people are the way they are? It's all part of the mystery of life, of being human.

The acclaimed feminist Eve Ensler said it best. She revealed that she was abused and assaulted by her father throughout her childhood. With the onset of the Me Too movement and the agony of trying to understand and dissect her father's behavior, she told Time Magazine, "I cannot explain why these men did what they did. I've given way too many years analyzing their perverse psychology, and I've exhausted every option. I no longer given a damn."

## You don't know where you stand with a lot of them

Some people are naturally transparent, and you know exactly where you stand with them and how they feel about you. Others, not so much. The best thing to be is yourself. Remember the popular phrase, "Those who matter won't mind and those who mind don't matter."

I have some relatives who aren't particularly friendly. I don't know if there's something going on with them or if it's more directly related to how they feel about me. It's understandable to occasionally wonder what they think about you. But we can easily read too much into this. You can interpret one of their gestures, expressions, comments, or messages in a few different ways. They may be judgmental, or not. They may have good intentions, or not. We just don't know; we need to embrace the mystery and be okay with not knowing.

Is the relationship important enough to you that you'll go ahead and make the effort to ask? If you're not going to ask and will be making an assumption, it's always better to give people the benefit of the doubt and make a positive assumption. Wayne Dyer said, "What other people think of me is none of my business." I'm not sure I agree with that 100%, as sometimes it's important to know. Olin Miller's quote, "You'll worry less about what people think about you when you realize how seldom they do," is more helpful.

Most people are preoccupied and self-absorbed. They're involved with their own mental noise and are not as focused on you as you may think. Make the assumption that's best for your peace of mind and to prevent people from getting in your headspace. If someone didn't respond to something you said, maybe he didn't hear you. If they haven't replied to a message, maybe they haven't received or read it yet. If they didn't say hi or acknowledge you, perhaps they didn't recognize or remember you.

The innocent explanation should be the default until proven otherwise. Maybe the way they're acting is more about them than about you. The acronym QTIP— quit taking it personally— applies. We can easily exhaust ourselves trying to mindread and figure out motives and intentions.

The speculation and wasted energy that goes on in the workplace is outrageous. With all these coworkers who we give too much energy to, ask yourself: If you suddenly passed away tomorrow, how many of them would bother to show up for your services? Probably not many, so they're not worthy of your mental space.

We don't need to know what people are thinking. We don't need to know what people are saying. To *need* to know is too exhausting. The best mindset is, "I have no idea what that person thinks about me and I'm fine with that." Remember, wolves don't concern themselves with the opinions of sheep.

## Not everyone's normal

Another key reminder is: Not everyone's normal. "Normal" is subjective. Who's to say what's normal or isn't? Not everyone has the full capacity to be the way you'd like or expect him to be. Many people are challenged or are on the spectrum of nonphysical illness, and it's not readily apparent just by looking at them. Martha Stout tells us in her excellent book, *The Sociopath Next Door*, that one in 25 ordinary Americans is a sociopath. This means that they're bereft of a conscience and cannot feel guilt. They're not necessarily criminals. Many seem very charming and dynamic. But, on the inside, there is no human empathy or humanity. Some of the sociopaths in the world can be charismatic leaders who, for their own benefit, use their skills to lead people into destruction.

Some people are very adept at lying. Some people want something so much that they figure if they repeat the lie enough, with authority and veracity, it will either come true or enough people will believe them. The love of money is the root of all evil. There are people who will lie to investors, steal funds from charities, and feign illness to raise money for personal gain. Elizabeth Holmes, who claimed that her company could perform over 200 blood tests from a single finger-prick drop of blood, and Billy Mcfarland, who unabashedly sold reservations to rent luxury condos that didn't exist on a remote island while promoting the fraudulent Fyre music festival, come to mind.

There are zealots who aren't in touch with reality. When you attempt to explain reality to intense or overconfident people who are blind to it, some will accuse you of being negative, part of the problem, and not a team player who looks for solutions. Some problems have no solutions; they're just bad ideas that aren't going to work. The most insecure people are the ones who only want people around them who agree with them and praise them.

There's too much gray area in our society to what fact, truth and reality is. Physics is fact, truth and reality. Gravity is f act, truth and reality. Would we ask someone if he believes in gravity? Why do we need to ask someone if he believes the earth is getting warmer?

There are people who are not worthy or your time or energy. We've got to pick friends that are deserving of us and reciprocate. Some people are takers, some are givers. Sometime the takers select the givers. Codependent relationships must be avoided.

I just imagine it as a statistical game. Returning to sociopaths, in a housing development with 50 neighbors, statistically at least two of the homes will be occupied by a sociopath. In a room of 100 random people, there'd be a predictable breakdown of both physical and mental health challenges and personality types. While mental illness is now acutely prevalent, not everybody has the correct diagnosis, treatment plan, or is taking the correct medication. Who know if there is any type of treatment for narcissism?

Therefore, expect it and see it as the norm, not the exception. Aberrations are the new normal. If you have a difficult colleague at your current position and you transfer elsewhere, so may your nemesis. He or she may have a different name or face. I use this strategy to help me not get so thrown off by others. Just say, "Okay, well, that's how that person is!" Sometimes what can define abnormal is that everyone around them can see their issues, but they have no awareness or acknowledgement of them. Most people just think they're wonderful. Many people lack emotional intelligence and the awareness of how they're perceived by others.

Don't expect everyone to be normal. Don't assume that people are intact. The Scout Law lists several positive traits. The reality of life is that not everyone is trustworthy, loyal, helpful, friendly, courteous, kind, obedient, cheerful, thrifty, brave, clean or reverent.

People are constantly showing us who they are. The best thing to do when people show you who they are is to believe them the first time. Don't give them five or six chances to disappoint you or impact your peace of mind. Fool me once, shame on you; fool me twice, shame on me.

## When you've been harmed

It's inevitable that others will hurt us since we're all human. That's being realistic. However, it's not healthy to go through life focusing on that since we don't want to attract it, look for evidence to back that up, or be preoccupied preparing for it. People seem to live up to and respond to the expectations we have for them. Some people who have been hurt become too guarded, go into protection mode, and won't allow themselves to be vulnerable for fear of being hurt again. Pain in life is inevitable, but misery is optional. Let's alleviate misery. Two great questions to ask yourself are:

1/ What can I do, that's under my control, to make things a bit better for myself?

2/ What things can I stop doing that accomplish nothing but

only make things worse than they already are?

From a mental toughness perspective, the best thing to do is feel the pain and express the pain. That's why they call it talk therapy. Hopefully you're validated so it will dissipate, and you'll have less of it with time. Support groups or a social network with people who have undergone what you're experiencing can be uplifting. You learn to stop replaying those situations and reliving the experiences. With a support system, your goal is to let go of the victim role.

There are several options to get negative emotions out of your system. Rage rooms, also known as smash rooms or anger rooms, have opened in cities around the world. They are a safe way to shatter away anger. You can hurl a plate across a room, take a sledgehammer to an old computer, or kiss a framed photo of an ex goodbye with a baseball bat. Some companies even have them on site to release counter-productive emotions and have more focus on work. At home, you can hang a bag and hit it with a stick or bat, like a piñata. You can buy cheap glasses and write all over them with a sharpie about the people or situations that frustrate you. You can then hurl these glasses into a recycling bin to get that satisfying smash.

Doing something physical dissipates cortisol that's stored in our body. Throughout most of human history we would do something physical, either fight or run, when our fight or flight response was triggered. Now, we just sit and stew.

Another option is to write someone a letter that you don't

intend to send. Really go off on them and get it all out. This gives you the chance to express without being judged. A variation of this is to write a second letter with what their reply would be in a best-case scenario, regardless of how unrealistic it is. This helps you to see the difference between how you'd like things to be and how they currently are; and to recognize that it's not in your power to merge the two versions.

You have the right to feel any way you want to feel. But how is it working for you and when is it time to quit? At some point, we need to get the emotions and feelings out of our system. Whatever works to find a way to turn the page, move on, and not let it linger.

Try to find ways to reframe things. You can tell yourself that there are no mistakes in life, only lessons; and you're stronger or better off for going through whatever was inflicted on you. You can incorporate what Richard Nixon said in his White House farewell speech: "Always remember, *others may hate you, but those* who *hate you don't win* unless you *hate them, and* then you destroy yourself."

I have a sister-in-law who had to deal with a frivolous lawsuit filed against her by one of my sisters to collect some money. It was eventually thrown out and determined that my sister had no legal basis to collect any money after a long process and painful trial. Yes, it was hurtful, stressful and expensive to have to deal with it. It's important to acknowledge that.

Eventually when we're dealing with others' issues, bitterness, insecurities or dysfunction, you have to look at it as a headspace game. The suit wasn't filed to win a legal victory or collect money, but rather to inflict harm and seek revenge, for whatever dysfunctional reason. I told my sister-in-law to not give her "opponent" the satisfaction of thinking about her at night and extracting her revenge by allowing her outposts in her head. She's just not worth it!

Another way to reframe situations is to say, "Things could be worse: I could be them." Or, "I'm so glad I don't have those issues." Or, "She's obviously very ill and living a dysfunctional life." If you can come up with something that makes you smile or gives you a chuckle, that's even better.

I recently got a call from my wireless provider to verify whether I had bought a new phone to be shipped to Alaska. "Of course not, I didn't do that!" was my reply. I was relieved they caught it and appreciative of their efforts to get the charge off my account. I was in a hurry and eager to answer the caller's questions. I forgot that I was the one being called; so they shouldn't need any of my info. Of course, they were trying to purchase several phones with the information I was giving them as they had me on hold. I stupidly gave them too much info to include my SS#. I have a friend who's' a personal security expert, and he helped me take the necessary steps to protect my credit. It just caught me off guard. He told me that I did what normal people do, and to chalk it up. But now I am on a "sucker list", so they will call, text and email forever. I need to be aware every time I am contracted in perpetuity. He also said that one percent of the population are human predators who live among us. They are criminals who are looking for victims. I think there are very few evil people in the world, but there certainly are a few. There are a lot more toxic people, or at least people who are toxic to us.

I needed to reframe this by thinking about how sad it is the way they live their lives. They're the ones who must live with themselves and their choices. I'm so glad I don't have to go through life that way. I'm not going to be giving them any more of my headspace.

Some of us have been subjected to unspeakable acts. Forgiving people who have harmed us protects our health and wellbeing. You don't forgive people for their benefit; you forgive people for your benefit. These quotes, while unattributed, are startling. "Forgiveness doesn't excuse behavior— forgiveness prevents behavior from destroying your heart." Also, "Not forgiving someone is like drinking poison and expecting the other person to die."

Mahatma Gandhi told us, "The weak can never forgive. Forgiveness is the attribute of the strong." Forgiveness is an attribute of the mentally tough. Not forgiving gives them too much space in your head. It's a process. It's vital to talk about the hurt so it doesn't turn into despair.

Forgive them so you don't let them define you.

# 14. Sleep

The number-one thing you can do to boost your overall health and performance is to sleep better. This is a reality that too many people haven't embraced or made a priority. There's a ton of research showing how poor sleep cripples the brain and body. Every bodily, mental, hormonal, or genetic impact you can think of is negatively impacted by poor sleep. Sleep is not a luxury or a lifestyle choice, it's a nonnegotiable biological necessity.

According to World Sleep Day statistics, sleep deprivation is threatening the health of up to 45% of the global population. There's also evidence that reduced sleep can cause genetic changes in your brain. A team from the University of Washington studied more than 1,700 twins and found those who regularly slept less than five hours a night have twice the risk for depression. They also found that too long or too short sleep durations activate certain genes related to depression.[30]

Just one night of poor sleep diminishes your cognitive output— the speed at which you process information. The neural pathways that allow information to travel smoothly to different parts of your brain are disrupted. Your decision making and problem solving aren't as effective. You're less useful to yourself and everyone around you. Your mood and your hormones become disrupted. According to a study from Stanford University, the level of one of these hormones, ghrelin, which stimulates feelings of hunger, jumps nearly 15 percent. The hormones estrogen and testosterone become reduced, and just about every other hormone is impacted.

Without adequate sleep, your brain is challenged to distinguish what's important and presents you with inaccurate and exaggerated internal fake news. Mental toughness and the ability to keep the negative thoughts at bay is more challenging since the noise is louder. Without good sleep, your resiliency, adversity quotient, and ability to bounce back from challenges is reduced. Instead of being like a bouncy rubber ball, you're more like a ball of slime that splats. It seems like there is so much more I have to figure out on the days I don't get a good night's sleep. I have to remind myself that I'm sleep deprived and cannot overreact or overanalyze anything.

The topic of sleep is all over the media and online worlds. The sleep-health industry is booming, collectively estimated to be worth around $40 billion. This comprises anything from monitoring apps, sound control, bedding, prescription sleep aids, sleep consultants, and more. I wish it was all due to awareness of sleep's impact on health, but I suspect a good deal of it is about being able to produce more. With all this information circulating about sleep, there are surprisingly many myths and misunderstandings.

Most of all, we really need between 7-10 hours of sleep each night, depending on our age. But the US Centers for Disease Control and Prevention states that a third of Americans sleep fewer than seven hours a night.[31] There is extensive evidence that consistently sleeping five hours a night or less greatly increases your risk for adverse health. People who reduced their sleep from seven to five hours or less a night were almost twice as likely to die from all causes, especially cardiovascular disease.[32]

Some people continue to think that five hours of sleep is fine, and the body and brain will adapt to this lower amount, but this isn't the case. And no, there's no amount of caffeine that can help you offset the negative impact of insufficient sleep.

We need to stop thinking that needing sleep is a sign of laziness or weakness. Some of us need to stop bragging about how little sleep we need or get. Some of us need to stop viewing less than average hours of sleep as something impressive, to be proud of, or evidence of their work ethic. If you insist on only getting close to five hours of sleep, you must accept that you're not going to live as long as you can, along with the other negative impacts. For some people, adding just one additional hour of sleep can provide tremendous all-around health benefits.

Most of us realize we sleep in stages or cycles. This is vital to remember since the quality of our sleep balances the quantity. Sleep cycles may have been an evolutionary protective characteristic, so we weren't vulnerable throughout the entire night.

The first stage is light sleep. In the second stage, we become disengaged from our environment, body temperature drops, and our heart rate slows down. We spend the most amount of time in the second stage.

Stages three and four are the deepest, most restorative stages. In stage three, also known as deep sleep, non-REM sleep, delta wave or slow-wave sleep, most physiological functions are markedly lower than in wakefulness. This is when muscles relax, neurons get a chance to rest, the supply of blood to the muscles increases, and the body repairs and grows tissue by releasing human growth hormone.

Stage four is rapid eye movement, or REM sleep. Your brain processes the day, stores memories, and regulates mood. There is a high level of brain activity with brain waves similar to when you're awake. This is when you dream. You don't toss or turn during this cycle because the muscles in your major extremities are paralyzed. This is so you can't move in response to your dreams. Sleep paralysis can happen for a few minutes if you're woken up before a REM cycle is finished. You'll be conscious, but the body's ability to move or speak hasn't been turned back on yet. There is so much going on that neurotransmitters fire, cortisol is released, and dreams become vivid and emotional. This isn't a relaxing period; it's an essential period. Stage four comprises roughly 25% of your total sleep time and can occur at any time. It usually begins about 90 minutes after you fall asleep.

We need to repeat the cycles four to five times to get a sufficient night's sleep and feel refreshed. Where and which cycle is disrupted greatly impacts grogginess and cognitive function.

For more effective sleep, avoid the obvious disruptors that are within your control, such as caffeine and alcohol after mid-afternoon. Avoid liquids altogether after a certain evening hour if that will cause your sleep to be disrupted.

Alcohol is not an effective sleep aid. Some people think it helps them sleep better since it can help you fall asleep faster. Alcohol destroys sleep quality by keeping the brain more locked into the lighter stages, so you don't wake up feeling rested and refreshed. REM sleep and the mental restoration that comes with it is particularly disrupted, causing daytime drowsiness, poor concentration, and a "hangover" feeling. The more you drink before retiring, the stronger the disruption. One or two standard drinks seem to have a minimal effect.[33]

If your breathing is interrupted during the night from a constricted airway, your brain will continually wake you from a lack of oxygen. This is devastating to your overall health. Loud snores followed by pauses in breathing is not normal and must be addressed. This dangerous sleep disorder, called sleep apnea, increases the risks for just about anything that can go wrong, from heart attacks, asthma, high blood pressure, atrial fibrillation, glaucoma, cancer, diabetes and kidney disease to cognitive behavior disorders. Sleep apnea usually goes undiagnosed. It's estimated to affect 30% of the population but only 10% have been diagnosed and are being treated. If you have it, you'll be exhausted and fighting all day long to not fall asleep. Falling asleep quickly during the day, like when a car or train starts moving, is a sign of someone who is exhausted, with a body grasping to repay its sleep debt. If you suspect that sleep apnea may be affecting you, or anyone has suggested it, then it's time to have a sleep study. CPAP (continuous positive airway pressure) machines are much smaller and less obtrusive than older models. Solving this problem has the potential to change every aspect of your life.

An inconvenient truth for many happens when the person they share a bed with disrupts their sleep. Issues can range from hogging the bedding, overheating, a restless leg, snoring, sleep talking, getting up a few times a night, and more. A study by the National Sleep Foundation found that almost a quarter of married couples have filed for a "sleep divorce", the act of having separate sleeping arrangements. Many others would like to but are apprehensive about bringing it up with their partner.[34]

Even if sleeping in separate rooms was a mutual decision, over 41 percent of Americans said they wouldn't admit it to their friends or family.[35] The preference for separate sleeping spaces has begun to affect home design. According to the National Association of Home Builders, there's been a steady increase in the number of requests for "two master bedroom" homes.

There's no shame in saying, "I love you but just can't sleep in the same bed overnight with you seven nights a week." Perhaps you could start off in the same bed but not remain there the entire night.

An adjustable mattress where you can control your own firmness and don't feel as much motion from the other side can work well, but sleeping in a separate bed can be the best thing for a relationship. When you're rested, you're a much better partner and easier to be around.

Another sleep disruptor happens because we're more connected to devices and more stimulated by them than ever. The blue light from the screens suppresses our melatonin production, a hormone which helps to regulate our internal body clock, or circadian rhythm.

There are settings on many devices to switch to a night shift at a specified time. This changes the light to a softer yellow, which has longer wavelengths than blue light. Reaching over to grab the phone a few times a night and getting a blast of blue light is disruptive to our sleep.

There are apps or devices you can get that will start to lightly glow at a certain time and become brighter to wake you up gradually. You can look over to see if it started to glow yet, and if not, go back to sleep and not worry about the time. Knowing what time it is stresses some people and they have a harder time falling back to sleep.

We can't watch something stimulating or read our work email in bed and expect to quickly fall asleep after turning it off. It works better for me to read something in paper form to fall asleep. I don't read anything on current events before bed or anything else upsetting or thought provoking. I choose neutral topics like entertainment news or movie reviews. A talk show or stand-up comedy without compelling action scenes works best. Crossword puzzles or anything non-stimulating that gives my brain something neutral to focus on works.

There is so much sleep advice out there and everyone has his opinions. Find a routine that works for you. I use a white noise machine, earplugs and a facemask. I've been told this makes me appear unapproachable. Some people find that an essential oil diffuser and lavender work well. First and foremost, go to bed at the same time every night and wake up at the same time every morning, even on the weekends. A cooler room will work better than a hotter one. Sleeping pills don't seem to produce naturalistic sleep. There are so many other natural remedies you can try.

An obvious sleep aid is to meditate and calm your nervous system and mind before retiring. Many people find a progressive body scan effective. You purposefully relax each extremity and body part you can think of. Tensing and holding each area for a few seconds then visualizing all the stress and tension leaving has you relax the body part. Visualizing that you are in a safe place, as in being snuggled in a black velvet hammock in a pitch-black room works for some.

Repeating a mantra or phrase, as in, "Don't think, don't think, don't think," can quickly induce sleep. One of the main reasons we can't fall asleep is our thoughts and noise. If we can stop them from getting momentum, we have a better chance.

Realistically, it's a struggle at times. If I'm physically tired but having trouble because my mind is racing, I'll do something similar to the subtraction exercise in Chapter 10— how to quiet the noise. I'll start with some random high number, as in 3,456 and keep subtracting seven from it. The math is difficult, takes a large amount of mental energy, and can facilitate falling asleep.

If it's just not working, or I'm not tired, I'm not going to just lay there. I'll get up and go to another room and do something mindless like a crossword puzzle. I don't want my brain to associate the bed with struggling or being awake; just like I don't want to associate a treadmill with standing. We don't sit at the dinner table waiting to get hungry and let ourselves become increasingly frustrated when we don't get hungry fast enough. It only makes things worse when we fret and snowball over the fact we're not sleeping. This only makes sleep less likely. It's ironic that, at the times when we believe we have a legitimate reason for having trouble falling asleep, we fall asleep faster since we're less judgmental of ourselves. Since most of it comes down to the story we tell ourselves about what's happening around us, or the 'spin' we put on things, find a good spin and story about your sleep.

Research reported on insomnia in the journal *Behavior Research and Therapy* found that identifying as an insomniac, complaining about sleep, and being stressed or guilty about your sleep can be a more important factor than the actual sleep you get! Oddly enough, researchers found that good sleepers, who objectively get enough sleep, but complain about their sleep and identify as insomniacs, exhibit comparable levels of daytime impairment as people with actual insomnia. Whether you got enough sleep or not, you wouldn't feel as much daytime impairment unless you reported high distress about your sleeplessness.[36] When it comes to getting rest, your "sleep self-appraisal takes precedence over sleep," the researchers concluded. When you think you're an insomniac, you help yourself become one. "When dread intermingles with sleep, the bedroom is a neutral or welcoming environment by day, a dystopia by night," the researchers warned.[37]

We've got to find a way to stop labeling ourselves as bad sleepers and reframe our sleep routine. When you catastrophize your bad sleep habits and beat yourself up about it, you're just making things worse. A great question to ask yourself is, "Can I be a normal sleeper if I'm not a perfect sleeper?" Sometimes when I find myself awake in the middle of the night for no apparent reason, I tell myself the following: "I must be coming off a successful deep-sleep cycle and now I'm at the lighter sleep stage. Soon I'll be back in a deeper cycle." It doesn't have to be a big deal and I don't need to make it dramatic.

You can find an app that works well for you. The Pzizz app works well for some. It launched in October 2016 and now has almost a million downloads across 160 countries. Whatever it takes. You must fight for, and demand, your sleep.

# 15.  Ask a Different Question

The most powerful thing we can do to diminish the negative noise is seek to find and then cherish our gratitude. The truth is we're all too blessed to be stressed. Too many of us don't realize this and are only looking for, and therefore only finding, what's wrong with ourselves and our lives.

Think of the target of your mental focus as a scale, like the third scale on page 147. On the far-left-hand side of this scale is focusing and dwelling on what is right or what you're grateful for this moment, your current life circumstances, or yourself in general. On the far-right-hand side is a mental focus of wanting things to be different or improved from how they actually are right now. If you are too far on the left-hand side, you may be overlooking opportunities to improve your life, or you may be lacking goals. If you are too far on the right-hand side, you're a perfectionist who finds something wrong in everything and you're never satisfied. For a healthy balance of living happily in the present moment tempered with motivating goals, we must be somewhere in the middle. Too many people are too far over on the right and succumb to the mindset of "I'll be happy when…"

The mindset of "I'll be happy when..." dilutes our appreciation for life and our blessings. Whenever we want something a certain way, in a way that we think will be better than it already is, we're in a losing battle. Let's be grateful for what we have, not focused on what's missing and what needs to be done.

We become what we think about most of the time. Not only does whatever we dwell or focus on become enlarged; we attract the experiences and people that correspond with our dominant thinking. Too many people don't know that gratitude transforms what we have into enough. Even more don't know that making the most of what we have turns it into more.

When you are focused on how your life can be improved, your mind is not in the present moment. When you're not in the present moment, your mind will continually think about how things can be improved, resulting in stress and anxiety. Even if you achieved what you think you want, you wouldn't be more content, because the same mindset that wants more now would want more later.

People who don't subscribe to the mindset of always wanting more or seeing happiness only in the future are the real enlightened ones. People who live the simplest lives, or lives that others may view as unsuccessful in a socioeconomic sense are, in many cases, the happiest. The place called "enough" is a very powerful place to be. When you feel as though you have enough, you can just stop and enjoy. How much is enough for you? Learning to be satisfied doesn't mean you can't, don't or shouldn't ever want more than you have, only that your happiness isn't contingent on it. Jim Rohn said, "Learn to be happy with what you have while you pursue all you want."

Happiness is not external; it's an internal feeling. It's feeling the greatest number of positive emotions. It doesn't matter what your status in life is or your material possessions. Some of the happiest people I've met are those who have the least. Some of the most dissatisfied were people who seem to have nothing to complain about.

I was in a popular deli that was crowded at lunch hour. Many of the patrons were professionals who seemed to be multitasking, impatient and annoyed with the wait for their sandwiches. The contrast with the workers behind the counter was striking. They genuinely appeared to enjoy what they were doing, and most were either humming, laughing or had a friendly banter going on with each other and the customers. They were efficient with their time and seemed to be focused on the present moment— the order they were working on. They didn't appear stressed about the others waiting in the line. The deli workers probably earn less than half the money that the annoyed customers earn. Part of the happiness equation should be the things you don't have to worry about. Most of the deli patrons were well off. They probably create many other things to worry and be dissatisfied about. So, who's really happier?

Some of us desperately need a shift in perspective. Some Americans should spend a few weeks in a Third World country. Too many of us don't realize that in some countries, the driving force in life is to obtain water.

One way to obtain more gratitude is to simply say thank you for what you have right now. Keep saying it until you mean it. If you say it long enough and with enough conviction, you will believe it. Every day is the third Thursday in November.

Another technique is to convince yourself that more isn't better, and that the problem doesn't lie in what you are lacking, but in longing for more. When thoughts of what would improve your life enter your mind, gently remind yourself that even if you got what you want, you will still not be satisfied with that mindset. Remind yourself of what you already have.

Another technique is to consciously change what you're looking for. We've all heard the phrase, "The grass is always greener on the other side." Why is that? Because that's how things look to you. Other people may look at your life with envy and see all kinds of awesome things. But you may not see those things. You may overlook or discount them or may be looking for something else.

Whatever you're looking for is exactly what you'll find. That's all that you'll see and what will grow bigger in your life. You'll exclude other things. Sir John Lubbock's quote, "What we see depends mainly on what we look for" says it all. No matter how well things are going, you can always find something that falls short of your expectations or falls short of being perfect. No matter how miserable you think your life is, you can always find something positive.

The good news is that you can boost your level of happiness

not by changing anything external, but by internally adjusting how you see things. How do we change what we're looking for? How do we see the splendor, the good things in our life? The answer is easy, and the day this resonates with you is a good day. What you do is simply ask yourself a different question.

How we feel at any given moment is a result of what we are focusing on, or what we see. What we are focused on is a result of what we are looking for. What we're looking for is a result of how we are evaluating things. How we are evaluating things is a result of what questions we are asking ourselves. We are constantly asking ourselves questions, and whatever questions we ask ourselves, our brains always find the answers to. Many people mistakenly ask themselves defeating questions such as: Why me? Why can't this place get their act together? Why can't these kids get themselves ready? Why does he/she have to be that way, …?

To change what you're looking for, start by writing out the answer to these questions:

1/ What am I grateful about in my life right now? Come up with at least five things.

2/ Then, taking each item one at a time, ask yourself: What about that, specifically, makes me grateful? List as many reasons as you can.

3/ How does that make me feel? Expand out the word "good" as much as you can.

It's a very simple but rare thing to do and can immediately change your emotional state. You could even be in a catastrophe and ask yourself, "What am I grateful about in my life right now?" The answer may be, "Nothing; everything is a disaster." If you slightly tweak the question and ask yourself, "What could I be thankful about in my life right now?" then you'll eventually get a different answer. Our brains will search all the files in the "hard drives" of our minds, or our subconscious minds, to find the answers. If you're stuck, start with the basics, such as your health.

Tony Robbins expands this concept with his "power questions". You ask yourself these questions in the morning and before you go to bed. Substitute as many words as you can think of for "thankful" and start the sequence over again. Some words to substitute can be "excited", "proud", "enjoying most", "committed to", etc. Examples could be, "What am I enjoying most in my life right now?" Or, "What am I excited about in my life right now?"

It's very effective to use the voice dictation button that's shaped like a microphone on smart phones and keep a running note going entitled "gratitude journal". I dictate about 5-10 things each day that I'm grateful for and want to savor. I may not do much with the note file, but it changes what I'm looking for. An example is on the next page.

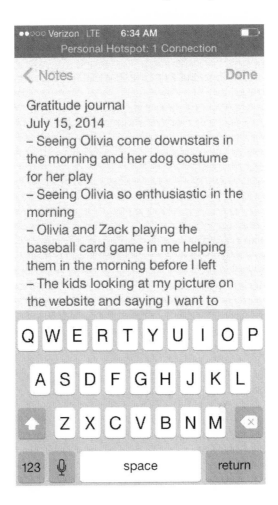

Personal Hotspot: 1 Connection

‹ Notes                                    Done

Gratitude journal
July 15, 2014
- Seeing Olivia come downstairs in
the morning and her dog costume
for her play
- Seeing Olivia so enthusiastic in the
morning
- Olivia and Zack playing the
baseball card game in me helping
them in the morning before I left
- The kids looking at my picture on
the website and saying I want to

Summation: Want to be happier? Change what you're thinking about and looking for. How do you change what you're thinking about and looking for? Ask yourself a different question. A better question.

# 16. Odds and Ends

## It's All About the Exhale

The common phrase "Take a breath" in order to relax is not going to give us the results we're looking for.

When you inhale, the sympathetic nervous system (fight or flight response) is activated. When you exhale, the parasympathetic nervous system (rest and digest) is activated. Both of these nervous systems are part of the autonomic nervous system, which is responsible for the involuntary functions of the human body; you don't consciously think about these things.

How you're breathing is critical information for the brain to know. If it's shallow or rapid, or if for some reason you're struggling to breathe, the locus coeruleus, located deep in your brainstem, sends signals out to the rest of your brain to put you on red alert, trigger anxiety and stress, and sharpen your reflexes as a survival mechanism. Conversely, if you exhale slowly, the locus coeruleus tells the rest of your brain that it's time to relax.

Researchers at Stanford University have proven how the ratio of inhaling to exhaling can be used to "hack" our brain into signaling that it's time to relax. Using genetic engineering on mice, researchers were able to isolate, and tried to disable, specific neurons that they thought regulated inhaling and exhaling. They initially thought the experiment had failed since, after the neurons were disabled, the mice still had the full scope of breathing abilities. But over the next few days they made an accidental discovery by observing that the mice were much calmer— grooming themselves even when put in new environments— which would normally trigger a stress response.[38]

What the researchers at Stanford realized was that the neurons they disabled simply report to the locus coeruleus on what's happening with your breathing, as a sort of spy. The same thing happens with us. Although the mice were sniffing and inhaling rapidly when put in new environments, their brains were not being told that. Therefore, there were no signals telling them to ramp up and get on high alert. The feedback cycle trigger that would cause more rapid breathing and heart rate was disabled, allowing them to remain calm.

The brain doesn't tell the body how to breathe unless it triggers the fight or flight response. Breathing simply is what it is, and our brain takes that input and responds to what is happening with breathing.

You can use your breathing to trick your brain into being calmer and altering your mood. It happens automatically, even if you're under stress. The most crucial part— you need to exhale for longer than you inhale. This can be done more easily by holding your breath for a few seconds before you exhale. Dr. Andrew Weil recommends inhaling with the nose for four seconds, holding that breath for seven seconds, then exhaling through the mouth for eight seconds. For me, holding my breath for seven seconds feels like an eternity, so I aim for four, four and eight.

If you do this for even a few cycles, it makes a tremendous difference. It's fascinating that the lungs and heart can feed back to the brain and essentially convince the brain that things are calm and peaceful, even when there are still stressful circumstances.

Deep breathing allows oxygen to fill the lungs, calms the mind, and relaxes muscles. This new respiratory cycle begins to slow the heart rate, sending a message to the brain that everything is more peaceful and calm than a few minutes ago. Our brains support this shift further by activating the rest and digest, or relaxation response that goes back from brain to body. This also means less cognitive thought activity, which is critical for when you're trying to sleep and need to calm the monkey mind. This is an amazing weapon in our arsenal to stay balanced and sane.

## Take a Nature Pill

Nature is nurture. The reduction of stress it provides is well established. Our growing indoor lifestyles dominated by screen viewing is harming us. It's not how we were designed. Far too many people are constantly glued to their screens, even when they're walking outside! They'd be hard-pressed to be mindful of, or notice, anything around them. I'm surprised more people don't have collisions with obvious barriers directly in their line of sight.

We now have the technology to measure biomarker levels

simply from saliva samples. This allows us to gauge how various experiences impact the body's hormone levels. A revealing study was done over an eight-week period where participants were asked to take a nature pill with a duration of 10 minutes or more, at least three times a week. During the nature experience, they could sit, walk, or do both. But there were a few rules they had to follow to minimize factors known to influence stress: take the nature pill in daylight, without aerobic exercise, and avoid the use of social media, Internet, phone calls, conversations and reading.

Levels of cortisol were measured from before and after saliva samples. The results from the data showed that just a twenty-minute nature experience, walking or sitting, was enough to significantly reduce the level of cortisol. If you spent a little more time, 20 to 30 minutes, immersed in the nature experience, the levels of cortisol levels dropped at their greatest rate. After 30 minutes, levels continued to drop, but at a slower rate.[39]

A nature 'pill' can be a great low-cost solution to mitigate the negative mental and physical health impacts stemming from all these electronics and urban living. The only side effects are a feeling of calmness and well-being.

Another study found that jogging outdoors makes people 50 percent happier than working out in a gym.[40] Remember, there's no Wi-Fi in the forest, but you will always find a better connection.

## Moods

Fluctuating moods are part of the human condition. Moods are like the tide; they flow in and flow out. Go with the flow of your moods and don't strain to resist the low ones. That just makes things worse and extends them. The lows can help you appreciate the highs and remind you that everything will pass.

The noise can precipitate depression. There are many times when it's helpful to resist, counter, or ignore the noise so it doesn't bring you down into a low mood.

There are times when you're better off to accept it and let it be. As Paul McCartney told us, "Speaking words of wisdom, let it be." The mood will pass sooner if you don't fight it and compound it with more chatter. Too many of us start to overanalyze and allow moods to create headlines or conclusions about our life. We think we're seeing things clearly, but we're not. Learn to question your judgement when you're in a low mood, how you're seeing things, and take everything with a grain of salt. That is not the time to draw conclusions or make major life decisions.

Sometimes we just have to leave things alone. Don't try to fix things. Don't feel bad or guilty. Just stay with it. Especially if you're tired or hungry, all bets are off. When I'm tired, it seems like there are pressing matters that must be resolved stat. That's seldom true.

Things will seem better in the morning. Accept that it will pass. It's okay to have a bad day. You don't need to assign a label to it, or yourself. We need to dial down the drama and dial up the perspective.

## Listen to the Noise

I've written much about ignoring the noise and viewing with prejudice. Sometimes the noise is valuable, and it can be trying to tell us something. Whatever you want to call it— the gut feeling, sixth sense, intuition, or voice in the background, it can hold important information.

When you're feeling conflicted or frustrated, that can be a good thing because that's when change happens. It doesn't happen when everything is rosy. Sometimes it takes getting fed up.

You'll grow if you ask what your emotions are trying to tell you. This is key because, when we use general statements about symptoms as in "I'm stressed," it just pushes the message of the feelings aside and doesn't consider the cause. Anxiety or stress might have a more specific message that can propel you forward. For example, "I'm resentful because I'm the only person among my siblings doing any caregiving for my parents. I need more help and support. I want each of my siblings to commit to two shifts a week."

By tuning in to the message of the emotion, you can achieve clarity and make better decisions. Like the snowball melt, writing things down can be helpful. Putting the message on trial and deciding how the evidence weighs will determine if the message is legitimate, or the usual garbage that the brain creates due to its negativity bias.

Stuffing our feelings with food, alcohol or any other kind of self-medicating is not healthy. Repression leads to depression. That little voice needs to be respected and listened to. Yes, there can be a signal in the noise.

## Find the Humor

We all know how beneficial laughter is. Children can laugh hundreds of times a day. Adults laugh significantly less because life tends to be more serious.

To motivate us to seek out more humor in our life, it's helpful to look at the scientific truth to the assertion laughter is the best medicine, along with physical changes in our body that laughter induces.

High blood pressure, or hypertension, is one of the most lethal side effects of stress and is a main risk factor for stroke and heart disease. It's known that mental or psychological stress causes the tissue that forms the inner lining of blood vessels, known as the endothelium, to constrict, reducing blood flow.

Stress is lowered through laughter. Laughter stops distressing emotions like anxiety, anger and sadness. There's also been research and investigation on whether laughter can lower blood pressure. The answer is a resounding yes. In fact, many studies, including one from the Maryland School of Medicine, has shown that laughing has the opposite effect on the endothelium, causing it to expand or dilate which increases blood flow. Laughter also enhances your intake of oxygen-rich air, stimulates your lungs, heart, and other muscles, along with prompting the brain to release endorphins. This is similar to what happens during exercise. A nice belly laugh fires up and then cools down your stress response, resulting in a good, relaxed feeling. Laughter also helps to ease pain by causing the body to produce its own natural painkillers and helps to reduce some of the physical symptoms of stress.

The success of laughter studies on blood pressure and other ills has led to a unique kind of treatment known as laughter yoga. In laughter yoga, people practice laughter as a group. Laughter is initially forced, but it can soon turn into spontaneous laughter. Laughter is contagious; just hearing it primes your brain and readies you to smile and join in the fun. You are much more likely to laugh around other people than when you're alone.

Technology like video and podcasts on demand has made it easier to find the type of humor we like and make it a part of our routine. There are no excuses anymore— even the experience of being stuck in traffic can be transformed by a funny podcast.

In the workplace, humor is the essential grease that keeps the machinery flowing. A coworker who you share laughs with is priceless. Nothing reduces tension, enhances relationships, and diffuses anger or conflict faster than a shared laugh. Looking at the funny side puts problems into perspective and enables us to move on from confrontations without holding onto resentment or bitterness.

The ability to laugh easily and frequently is a tremendous resource for dealing with life's challenges. Best of all, this invaluable medicine is free, fun, and easy to use. Look for humorous situations and surround yourself with reminders to lighten up. When was the last time you had a belly laugh?

## Exercise

Our bodies are machines. All machines require maintenance. People ignore this. Maintenance takes time, at least a few hours a week. We need to work up a sweat a few times a week with some form of cardio exercise. There's also a direct correlation between aging out of place and strength training.

Public health guidelines state we need at least 150 minutes of moderate exercise or 75 minutes of vigorous exercise per week. High-intensity exercise releases endorphins, resulting in the runner's high that joggers report. Reams of data support the beneficial health effects of hitting this goal. Schedule everything else around exercise, prioritize and protect it.

Human beings evolved to move. Our bodies, including our brains, were fine-tuned for endurance activities over millennia of stalking and chasing down prey.

Guidelines also suggest doing "strength-promoting exercise" at least twice a week. Numerous studies show if you have sufficient muscle strength, not necessarily muscle mass, you live longer.

For most of us the real value is in low-intensity exercise sustained over time. This kind of activity spurs the release of proteins called neurotrophic or growth factors, which encourages the growth of new brain cells and helps existing ones to grow and make new connections. The resulting improvement in brain function makes you feel better. Neuroscientists have determined that in people suffering with depression, several areas of the brain, including the hippocampus, which helps to regulate mood, are smaller. Exercise supports nerve cell growth in the hippocampus, improving nerve cell connections, which helps relieve depression. It also strengthens our biochemical resilience to stress and bolsters our self-esteem. It allows you to say, "Look at what I just accomplished and the strength and endurance I have. This is something positive about myself." For most people with mild to moderate depression, exercise is one of the most effective, affordable, practical, and enjoyable treatments available. The beneficial form of physical stress that exercising places on the body appears to make us more resistant to psychological and mental stress.

For the severely or clinically depressed, the last thing they want to do is to get up or move. It can be a vicious cycle. Am I lying in bed from depression, or am I depressed since I'm not being active?

To get up and go is sometimes the hardest thing to do. A journey of a thousand miles begins with a single step. We've got to give ourselves a chance to succeed by setting up an environment where it's easier to do hard things. Perhaps even wearing running attire to bed, since if you're already dressed all you need to do is to walk out the door. Even ten minutes of exercise is better than none.

## Determine Your EYOD to Live With More Life

Life is a temporary journey. We don't know when it's going to end. All we have is the journey. There is no destination that we will arrive to where everything is ideal and without frustration. We can make the journey more meaningful by being more mindful that it has an ending. That's completely normal. It's both expected and inevitable. Sometimes the expected happens sooner than expected. Either way it's going to happen. Why not use this fact to enhance today?

One way to make your life more meaningful is to determine your EYOD, or expected year of death. You simply subtract your current age from the average life expectancy for your gender and country to determine the number of years you should have left. You then add that to the current year. My EYOD is 2053. Knowing this number is a good reminder on how limited my time is and motivates me to make the most of it.

We've also got to be mindful that's if we're lucky— if we make it to our EYOD. If we're lucky we live to a ripe old age. There are no guarantees. What is the quality of old age?

Anyone who has lost someone close suddenly understands that life can stop on a dime. Close to where I live, an elementary school art teacher was recently on her way to work driving on a highway. Somehow, a 200-pound manhole cover on the roadway became dislodged and flew through the windshield of her car, killing her. We never know how much time we have left. Here's the eternal question: Should we be living as if we'll live forever, or should we be living as if every day could be our last?

Life should be like a sandcastle. We ought to enjoy the process of making it and embrace the impermanence that the tide will gradually come in and reclaim it. To enjoy it, we've got to be in the present moment.

Our brains easily trick us out of the present with distorted memories that make the past seem better than it was, and with anticipating an idealized future. There are so many future unknowns. It does us no good to be engaging with them.

Since I don't know how much time I have left, I'm borrowing another song lyric as my mantra. This one comes from the Whitesnake song, "Here I go again." That lyric is: "I've made up my mind, I ain't wasting no more time."

To stop wasting time and energy don't worry about thinking only good thoughts. That would be exhausting and all-consuming. What we need to do is simply embrace only good thoughts.

After all, only humans regret the past, worry about the future, and find fault with, make comparisons about, and blame ourselves for the present. We forget that all of us think so differently, and our inner worlds are all so diverse. What one person views as repulsive, another might find enjoyable. But we get frustrated when we can't get what we want, and upset when what we like comes to an end. We suffer over the fact that we suffer.

This kind of suffering— which comprises most of our discontent, unhappiness and frustration— is manufactured by the brain. It is made up, which is ironic, poignant, and extremely encouraging. The bottom line is this: To change how we feel, we must change how we think. The quality of your thinking determines the quality of your life. What do you think?

# 17. Notes

1. Foreman, Kyle J, PhD. "Global Health Metrics: Forecasting Life Expectancy." *The Lancet.* 2018; 392: 2052–90

2. Creese, Andrew; Gasman, Nadine, and Mariko, Mamadou; "The World Medicines Situation." World Health Organization, 2004

3. Fulenwider, Anne. "Reese Witherspoon Is Leading the Charge." *Marie Claire,* March 2018

4. Thompson, Wright. "The Mastermind." *ESPN the Magazine* 9/20/16.

5. Centers for Disease Control and Prevention (CDC). "Selected prescription drug classes used in the past 30 days, by sex and age: United States." https://www.cdc.gov/nchs/data/hus/2016/080.pdf

6. American College Health Association. Spring 2017 survey

7. Liu, Cindy, Ph.D, and Foreman, April, Ph.D. *Depression and Anxiety,* online, Sept. 6, 2018.

8. Matthews, Melissa and Phelps, Michael. *Men's Health,* October 26th 2018

9. Beck, Taylor. "A vaccine for depression? Ketamine's remarkable effect bolsters a new theory of mental illness." *Nautilus.* December 17th, 2015.

10. Perry, Mo. "Wellness from Within." *Sky Magazine.* February 2018.

11. Belluck, Pam. "F.D.A. approves first drug for postpartum depression." *New York Times.* March 19th, 2019.

12. Killingsworth, Matthew and Gilbert, Daniel. "A Wandering Mind Is an Unhappy Mind." Science. 12 Nov 2010: Issue 6006, pp. 932

13. Gibbons, Ann. "The Human Family's Earliest Ancestors." Smithsonian Magazine. March 2010

14. Harari, Yuval Noah. "Sapiens- a brief history of Humankind." HarperCollins. New York, NY. February 2015.

15. IBID

16. White, Matthew. "Worldwide Statistics of Casualties, Massacres, Disasters and Atrocities." *The Historical Atlas of the Twentieth Century.*

17. Helmstetter Shad, Ph.D. "What to Say When you Talk to Yourself." Simon and Schuster. New York, NY. 1986

18. Begley, Sharon. "How the Brain Rewires Itself." *Time Magazine.* Jan 19th 2007

19. Bajarin, Ben. "Apple's Penchant for Consumer Security." *Techpinions.com.* April 18, 2016

20. "The Facebook Experiment." *The Happiness Research Institute* 2015.

21. Hölzel, Britta K. and Lazar, Sara W. "Mindfulness practice leads to increases in regional brain gray matter density." National Center for Biotechnology Information/ US National Library of Medicine/ National Institutes of Health. PMCID: PMC3004979

22. Sundquist, Jan. "The effect of mindfulness group therapy on a broad range of psychiatric symptoms: A controlled trial in primary health care." *European Psychiatry.* Elsevier Publishing. June 2017.

23. Balter, Michael. "Why Einstein Was a Genius." *ScienceMag.Org.* 11/15/02

24. Lazar, Sara W., Kerr, Catherine E. and Wasserman, Rachel H. "Meditation experience is associated with increased cortical thickness." National Center for Biotechnology Information/ US National Library of Medicine/ National Institutes of Health. PMCID: PMC1361002

25. Wieth, Mareike B and Zacks, Rose T. "Time of day effects on problem solving: When the non-optimal is optimal." *Thinking & Reasoning.* Volume 17, 2011. Issue 4, 387-401.

26. Hanson, Rick Ph.D. "Hardwiring Happiness: The New Brain Science of Contentment, Calm, and Confidence." Penguin Random House LLC, New York. 2013

27. McCraty, Rollin and Zayas, Maria. "Cardiac coherence, self-regulation, autonomic stability, and psychosocial well-being."
Frontiers in Psychology. 2014; 5: 1090. PMCID: PMC4179616
doi: 10.3389/fpsyg.2014.01090

28. Moore, Michael Scott. "PTSD brain studies look at the hippocampus."
Pacific Standard Magazine. July 6, 2011.

29. Blasey-Ford, Christine, Ph.D. Senate Judiciary Committee Testimony.
September 27th, 2018.

30. Watson, Nathaniel F., MD. "Sleep Duration and Depressive Symptoms: A Gene-Environment Interaction" PMCID: PMC3900629

31. Centers for Disease Control and Prevention.
https://www.cdc.gov/sleep/data_statistics.html

32. Ferrie, Jane E., Ph.D. "A Prospective Study of Change in Sleep Duration: Associations with Mortality in the Whitehall II Cohort." US National Library of Medicine; National Institutes of Health; PMCID: PMC2276139

33. Ebrahim, Irshaad. Alcoholism: Clinical & Experimental Research. April 2013

34. Carlson, Marten. "Almost Half of Americans Want the Bed to Themselves." Mattress Clarity. September 18th, 2018

35. National Sleep Foundation. "Sleep in America Polls."
https://www.sleepfoundation.org/professionals/sleep-america-polls

36. Torres, Monica. "Believing you're an insomniac may be costing you sleep and productivity." The Ladders. October 27, 2017

37. Lichstein, Kenneth L. "Insomnia Identity." Behavior Research and Therapy. Volume 97, October 2017, Pages 230-241

38. Goldman, Bruce. "Study shows how slow breathing induces tranquility." Stanford University School of Medicine News Center. March 2017.

39. Hunter MaryCarol R.; Gillespie Brenda W.; Yu-Pu Chen, Sophie.

"Urban Nature Experiences Reduce Stress in the Context of Daily Life Based on Salivary Biomarkers." *Frontiers in Psychology*, 2019; 10

40. Cramb, Auslan. "Jogging in forest twice as good as trip to gym for mental health." Telegraph UK Health News. June 2012.

41. Miller, Michael M.D. "School of Medicine Study Shows Laughter Helps Blood Vessels Function Better." Maryland School of Medicine News Release.

# About TrainRight, Inc.

## Train**Right**, Inc.
### Training the *right* way

TrainRight, Inc. is a professional education and consulting firm providing customized training programs, coaching initiatives, keynote presentations and group seminars. We specialize in eliminating self-created problems and distractions that impede productivity and developing the cognitive skills of focus, concentration, creative problem solving, and critical and positive thinking. We assist our clients with individual effectiveness, sales resiliency, conflict resolution, time management, stress management, team building, professional and effective workplace communications, leadership development, coaching and feedback.

At TrainRight, we get under the surface to figure out why people do what they do and why what they do makes sense to them. We show people what it costs them personally and professionally when they continue on the current course. We are motivational catalysts to help people implement change from the inside out and teach the practical skills needed to implement and sustain new behavior patterns. The participants in TrainRight's sessions discover how to reframe their challenges to see real changes and results. TrainRight has a proven record of helping organizations enhance their environment and productivity.

For more information, visit www.trainrightinc.com or call 1-800-603-7168; or email: info@trainrightinc.com

# About Kevin Stacey

Kevin Stacey, MBA, is an effectiveness expert, author, and former brain imaging specialist who enhances performance, boosts resiliency, and accelerates results. He combines his military background, management training, experience as a healthcare clinician, and successful manager at the nation's largest managed care company to be a catalyst for workplace improvement. After starting his medical career at Walter Reed Army Medical Center, Kevin brings the principles of neuroscience into the modern business world to effect change from the inside-out. He works with organizations and leaders to help them become more effective, productive and profitable. He helps people overcome the brain's inherent negativity bias, even-out the playing field, and realize it's not more business acumen that's going to make the difference and boost performance; it's managing your biology— specifically your brain. His programs provide concrete information and practical solutions for business problems. Kevin's knowledge, experience, warm demeanor and sense of humor create a human connection that motivates people to make positive changes and assume personal responsibility for their circumstances.

Kevin has a proven record of helping organizations enhance their environment and productivity. From IBM to The New York Times, Ford Motor Company, JP Morgan Chase, Bayer, Goody Hair Care, United Technologies, Boeing, and Sara Lee, he has worked with the world's best and brightest. His services help these and other clients achieve increased performance, sales, higher employee retention, greater job satisfaction, and improved service quality. He is CEO and founder of TrainRight, Inc., with a highly-skilled team of facilitators offering programs globally. For more info: www.KevinStacey.com